From Mary Cardaras

adoption survivor: Dena was taken from her Greek biological parents in 1958, but she found her way back to the village after many years. Her transatlantic adoption strikes home how intercountry adoption has affected all parties involved: the first family, the extended new family, the struggling young couple, their children, the village community back in Greece. Told with deep empathy and real *couleur locale*, Mary Cardaras, a searching Greek adoptee herself, tells an intimate personal story with a recognizable global dimension. The result has us confirm that truth is, after all, more gripping than fiction.

   Gonda Van Steen,
Koraes Chair of Modern Greek and Byzantine History, Language and Literature, King's College, London
Author of *Adoption, Memory and Cold War Greece: Kid Pro Quo?*

What a beautiful but tragic story of love and resilience! Cardaras's telling of Dena's story is exquisitely balanced between the challenges that Dena lives versus the enduring love between her Greek parents, who were never supported and had little to hope for. This novella brought tears to my eyes because it resonated within and is sadly the experience of too many of us. It is so true that as adopted people, we live a lifetime of pain in never knowing who we fully are, until we find our origins, our beginnings, the answers to our questions. I highly recommend this book for any adoptee, who has suffered in their adoption, who searches for their origins and dares to hope. For others, Cardaras has done a fantastic job bringing this story together to highlight the true human tragedy resulting from the sale and trafficking of children in adoption.

   Lynelle Long
Founder and Executive Director, Intercountry Adoptee Voices
Author of *The Colour of Time: A Longitudinal Exploration of Intercountry Adoption in Australia*

With searing detail and lean, crisp prose, in "Ripped at the Root" Mary Cardaras tells the story of Dena Polites, a woman born to a young unwed Greek couple who was adopted by married Greek Americans in Ohio. Polites's tale serves as a focal point for the some 4,000 Greek infants and children who, in the years after World War II, were torn from their families, country, culture and dispatched to live with distant strangers in the US and Western Europe. In the midst of the Cold War, these children—many the sons and daughters of Greek leftists—became pawns in the global battle for democracy. In this powerful, un-put-downable narrative, Cardaras gives voice not only to Greek adoptees, but to international adoptees everywhere as they navigate returns to their birthplaces; their birth relatives; and reclaim their stolen origin stories.

Gabrielle Glaser
Journalist and best-selling writer
Author of *American Baby*

Drawing from the personal testimonies of a Greek American adoptee and her extended family, Mary Cardaras brings to life the personal and social dramas surrounding the quest for one's biological parents. This is an engrossing narrative piercing family secrets and piecing together fragments of this puzzle-like adoption story. Cardaras plots a fascinating microhistory which connects personal experience with broader processes of deception, betrayal, illegality, but also steadfast devotion and commitment. From this angle, this is not merely an adoption story, but a story that does not shy away from dissecting difficult truths about the social realities of immigrant and American ethnic life.

Yiorgos Anagnostou
Modern Greek Program
Ohio State University

In rural Greece, despite or perhaps of the huge value of the family as a social unit, a cultural hostility toward childbirth out of wedlock generated unusually large numbers of children put up for adoption. The regular occurrence of wars from the early 19th to the mid-20th centuries made things even worse. The adoption processes led to happy outcomes but also unhappy ones, especially when it was forced or imposed against the mother's wishes. But even in those cases, as Mary Cardaras demonstrates in this dramatic and emotionally crafted narrative, the drive to find one's roots along with human perseverance and goodness can ultimately prevail.

Alexander Kitroeff
Professor of History
Haverford College

Heartbreaking yet hopeful. Mary Cardaras brings a tragic injustice to light that deserves the world's attention and action so that thousands of Greek-born adoptees from the late 1940's to the 1960's, who were also ripped at the root, may once again blossom.

Gregory Pappas
Publisher and Founder
The Pappas Post

What a wonderful and riveting story! Mary Cardaras brings to life the story of Dena Polites, born in Greece and adopted to a family in Ohio, whose life trajectory leads to searching for and reclaiming her own cultural identity. Cardaras, a Greek intercountry adoptee herself, captures the complex pathos and heartbreak of intercountry adoption and the history of what happened to thousands of Greek children and the parents who relinquished them to adoption during the Cold War. It is a tale, based in real-life, that captures every adoptees' yearning to know who you are and how you came to lead a second and fundamentally different life. A great read. Brava!

Greg Luce
Adoptee Rights Law

Ripped at the Root
AN ADOPTION STORY

Based on True Events

Mary Cardaras

SPUYTEN DUYVIL

NEW YORK CITY

© 2021 Mary Cardaras
ISBN 978-1-956005-27-1

Cover Design by Lisa Saper & T Thilleman

Library of Congress Cataloging-in-Publication Data

Names: Cardaras, Mary, 1955- author.
Title: Ripped at the root : an adoption story / Mary Cardaras.
Description: New York, NY : Spuyten Duyvil, [2022] | "Based on true
    events"--Title page. |
Identifiers: LCCN 2021039898 | ISBN 9781956005271 (paperback)
Subjects: LCSH: Intercountry adoption--Greece--History--20th century. |
    Adoptees--Biography. | Cardaras, Mary, 1955-
Classification: LCC HV875.58.G8 C37 2022 | DDC 362.734092
    [B]--dc23/eng/20211012
LC record available at https://lccn.loc.gov/2021039898

Dedicated to the lost children of Greece...
who are still searching for home.

Ripped at the Root: An Adoption Story is a true story. It is based wholly on primary source material. The dialogue was created based on conversations that were either actually spoken by the subjects or overheard and recounted. Many of the images of various parts of Greece, village life, and the zeitgeist of the times they reflect, which are painted in the narrative, have been recounted and described by the subjects and experienced by the author herself. No names have been altered. Neither have the names of any places.

"The LORD is close to the brokenhearted
and saves those who are crushed in spirit."

—Psalms 34:18

It was lust at first sight.

They watched each other from across the dance floor. While one looked away, the other would steal a glance. It was a flirtatious-inspiring environment to be sure. Their eyes would finally meet. They lingered, shy smiles would emerge, then a spark, chemistry, and the sweet beginnings to a fusion of souls. Their attraction was like the pull of magnets. There was an inevitability in their match. The intoxication of music would also further prod destiny.

The sky was overture to their eventual union. They began under a carpet of stars against a black night sky. Above crowded, tiny, shimmering jewels, gently pulsating above a remote Greek village. The hamlet was gently tucked away in the Pindus mountains, which is in the orbit of the larger Ioannina, once a city for silversmithing, in the far north of the country. Unless you have any specific reason to go, it is a region of Greece less traveled and off the beaten track.

This place was life and home to one Vasiliki Gyftokosta and Apostolos Papazacharis.

Their mountain home, the village of Kastania, is located just a stone's throw from the Albanian border to the north and hours from a bigger city anywhere in Greece. It had a church, a touchstone for the village, of course, because what Greek village doesn't. It had several *kafeneia*, coffee-houses, where men met to be men together, as the synchronized click-click of their worry beads punctuated the silences between conversation and laughter.

The village had a central, small *plateia*, a village square, where people came together to shop and gossip, to retrieve water from the *vrisi*, the communal fountain, and where women brought their bread to the town *fourno*, an oven for the entire community, like a kiln, so as not to needlessly heat up the house, especially in summer. Kastania had a grocery store for some necessary provisions that could not be grown or raised on the surrounding land.

Thick and durable greystone houses with worn and faded terracotta-tile roofs dotted the hills. The twisted mountain roads were difficult to navigate by car because of the switchbacks and steep terrain. Rocky and dusty, they are lined with evergreen trees and weave through and around blankets of wild, dry brush. Swaths of rugged groves of olive and chestnut trees blanket the land. Their ancient and gnarled, exposed roots swell up from the soil like the veins on the feet of an old man. Unkempt grass and brittle ground cover lay like skirts around the trees. The hidden, ever-present cicadas provided nature's persistent symphony during the summer nights.

This was Kastania. The year was 1957.

It was where and when 22-year-old Vasiliki and 21-year-old Apostolos actually met. They had known *of* each other. Maybe even *seen* each other in passing, but without any focus. It was a small village, but big enough that a shy someone might be indistinct. Ultimately, it would be the music and the dance floor that would bring them to notice one another, to see each other, and to put into focus, each for the other.

She was a girl from a poor family, the eldest of seven siblings, the daughter of Giorgos, a *tsangaris*, a cobbler, whose work was to make and mend shoes. Her mother, Constantina, was a homemaker and wife. Seven children in a poor village was quite enough for her to manage.

He was one of five siblings, the youngest and only boy among a doting mother, Penelope, and a gaggle of attentive sisters. His family was much better off, by Greek village standards. His stern, authoritarian father, also named Giorgos, was very strict and a difficult, complicated man. Hardened. He was an *agrotis*, a farmer, but he was also a *chorafias*, a land-owner, which gave him some standing in the small community. Compared to the Gyftokostas family, the Papazacharis clan had some wealth and assets thereby giving it some stature. And because of that, they may have been respected by the other villagers—or not.

Giorgos Papazacharis would never approve of any relationship his son might cultivate with Vasiliki, or anyone like her. A girl from a poor family could provide little to no *prika*, a dowry. This was a prerequisite of the time and essential for marriage. A groom must be able to provide, but a bride and future wife must bring something to the nuptial table.

Vasiliki had little to nothing materially to offer a marriage, as if her love for Apostolos and his for her were not enough. It would not, it could never be enough to suit Giorgos. Love need not necessarily factor into a marriage anyway, at least not in the beginning. This was an arrangement, a financial arrangement, and also a prelude to children, to building a family one could have pride in, and one that would be productive. She was from the other side of the tracks, so to speak, a woman ill-suited for the more prominent and proper Papazacharis family.

Vasiliki worked alongside her mother learning to cook, clean, and sew because women of that time and place were bred to be housewives and mothers. Apostolos helped his father in the fields and with the animals as a good and only dutiful son would do, and must do.

Apostolos was called Zacharis by his friends. He had a soft and romantic, lyrical side. The household of six women had some influence on him. He was the baby of the family and so grew to be a man of few words with a quiet and calm soul that was as deep and as dark as a hidden village well, overgrown with vines and brush. Like that well, he was barely noticed and hard to reach. But it was the music. That is what brought Zacharis alive inside and when people noticed.

He loved music and was attracted to the *clarino*, the clarinet. At eight years old he made himself a *flogera*, a flute, out of wood, and he bore the holes himself for his tiny fingers to make, at first, random sounds, and then the patterns of music. In Greek music, particularly in regional Epirus, it is the *clarino* that is often the heart and soul of any ensemble. It beckons. There is something about it; an alluring communication in notes and inflection that cannot be easily described. It touches the Greek heart to its core. It wails. It moans. It pokes and prods a place deep within. It is hypnotic. The clarinet seems to speak words that other instruments cannot, at least not as clearly. It takes the music to another, to a higher plane in the hearts of Greeks, who love their music and dancing. Both often expose the very soul of a person. Some have said that the *clarino* taps into a "primal well of emotion."

Zacharis was handsome, of average height, with a trim, but solid build. He had a distinctive, small mustache that marked his upper lip. It was fitting that he was drawn to the *clarino*. His instrument would speak the words, perhaps, that he could not, that he could never. He loved the *clarino* so much that he learned to play without instruction. Self-taught and disciplined, he soon became very accomplished.

Apostolos Papazacharis, young Zacharis, was in demand and serious about his music, always wanting to share it. He played with his small band at weddings and after baptisms; he played at Name Day celebrations, which in Greece are more significant than birthdays; at village *paniyiria*, festivals, and at any *glendia*, parties that celebrate Greek culture in any form, in any village. And so, he made the rounds and a name for himself at home in Kastania and in the other small surrounding villages.

Vasiliki was known to her friends and family as Vasilo. Pretty and dark-skinned, small, buxom, and sexy, she was full of life and easy to smile and laugh. She had a special spark, was funny and open, and she was a very good dancer. When she was not helping her mother at home, she was socializing with girlfriends, and where there was the opportunity to dance, she was dancing.

Vasilo attended one of the *glendia* at which Zacharis played. He may have seen her around the village, but it was while she danced that he took notice. She could not help but notice him. She loved the way he played, which perhaps expressed and exposed the depth of his soul, and later his attraction to her.

Vasilo loved to dance and with other villagers she danced to the sonic distinction of his artistry with the clarinet. She was enthusiastic about the traditional Greek line dancing as the wafting of the *clarino* drifted and bounded about in the thin mountain air, echoing off the stone houses, bouncing from mountain to hillside.

The *tsamiko*. She loved to dance the *tsamiko*.

Greek dancing. A hand holds the one next to it in line, arms bent at the elbow in a V- formation. Round and round at first, and then the line snakes in and out to wherever it is the leader takes it. It is that dancer, at the front of the line, who shares his or her *kefi* as they are often overcome by the music and their own feelings. Like a trance.

Kefi.

It is a concept almost indescribable. It is a feeling that emanates from deep inside one's heart. It is the pure joy one can feel. A love of living and of life realized. A lightness of being. Untethered from time and place. Free. And dancing can release that *kefi*, especially when a heart is full, and if it meets the heart of another that is watching.

Kefi.

It is what Vasilo felt whenever she danced to the music of Zacharis. Others always urged her to dance at the front of the line. She was an artful, soulful Greek dancer. All who watched her were captivated when Vasilo took the lead.

The couple's relationship began discreetly. She began to follow him to wherever he played and, naturally, they flirted with each other. Essentially, she was a groupie of the times. In villages around Kastania, when Zacharis and his band took a break they would steal some time away to talk, to kiss, to feel each other, and eventually to get to know one another while sharing stories about their lives.

The lust of the young lovers was like kindling, fueling their budding relationship. It was made even more passionate by being forbidden to couple, and they knew it. They were forced to be secretive, to hide. Their love grew without witness or support. Star-crossed, their hearts grew closer, fused to the notion of maybe, someday making a life together. But their situation was fraught with difficulty and challenge.

It happened on one of these nights near their home village of Kastania under a wondrous night sky. It was at the base of a tree in a field dotted with walnut and chestnut trees. Their branches threw a bed of shadows, deeper cover, and seclusion for discreet lovemaking. This is where their daughter was conceived; a night they would always remember for it was all they had, and all they would have for years.

The pregnancy was a secret until it was impossible to keep. Vasilo would eventually tell her father, a warm and understanding man, whom she adored and trusted. She had no choice *but* to tell him, and in a small village where news cannot be kept secret for long, of course, it got out and was circulated. Vasilo was a scandal in the village. She was an embarrassment. Not to her family, but to others the family knew.

Ntropi. It is the Greek word for shame. It can be overwhelming in a small minded, clannish environment like Kastania. And in those times.

It was Zacharis's father, Giorgos, who said he would not tolerate such a child or any kind of union between the couple. "You will not have this child," he told his son. "Take care of it," he said coldly and with finality, pointing a finger at his face. It was code, of course, for an abortion or to abandon, disavow Vasilo and his own child.

As Vasilo's belly expanded, Giorgos became more enraged. He even confronted her directly, intimidating her, demanding that she leave the village, the only home she knew. "Do not come back. Not ever," he said with both venom and disgust. If she did return with "that child," his own grandchild, his blood, he told her he would "kill her," and he would "kill the baby," too. He threatened her with such raw, brazen anger that it drove her away, to be exiled miles from her village, and far from the place she loved. It also forced her away from her beloved Zacharis.

Vasilo and her mother, Constantina, left Kastania for the city of Arta, nearly 30 miles south, but a world away, where no one would know her and, hopefully, not judge her. It was there where she would grow taut and uncomfortable, waiting for her baby to come. It was there where her mother would support her while she brought her infant into the world. She worried and wondered.

What would she do after the baby was born? What would become of them?

In Kastania, with the love of his life driven away and now pregnant with his child,

Zacharis fell into a quiet despair. He wanted and needed independence from his father. He wanted his own money to spend as he pleased and with whom he pleased. His closest friends needed money as well. All were young men from a poor village and had few prospects.

One night they were drinking together and had too much. They became raucous. Wound-up. On a dare, they challenged the unassuming Zacharis. "If you really need and want your own money to get out from under your father's thumb," they said with swagger, "we know someone who has money hidden in his house. Come with us." So, they decided to rob an old man from their own village, who happened to have some money.

Zacharis was appointed to be the lookout as his two friends entered the house to take any money and valuables they could find. He waited, hidden in the shadows, feeling the effects of the drink. With his shirt sleeves rolled up, as he always wore them, he pulled smoke deep into his lungs from a cigarette he had rolled himself. It was quiet.

What was keeping his friends? When would they finally emerge so they could flee the scene of this petty, stupid crime? But they didn't exit the way they had entered. They had gone, leaving Zacharis stranded there by himself in the dark. He grew impatient.

After a last long drag on his cigarette, he flicked it to the ground, and rubbed it out. The sound of his shoe in the gravel seemed amplified in the dead silence of this night.

He was nervous, but Zacharis finally went in to search for them, to tell them to hurry it up. Time, it seemed, was running out.

Startled, what he did find was only the old man. He had crumpled to the floor. He looked so vulnerable and small, Zacharis thought, as he lay on his side. His eyes darted around the room. His friends. They were nowhere. His focus returned to the old man. Now he saw that blood was oozing from the side of his skull, a slow pool of dark liquid widening onto the wooden planks. Did he fall and catch his head on the table's edge? Had he lost his balance? Or worse. Did his friends strike him? Did they do this?

Zacharis's heart began to pound. He was breathing heavily now as he shook himself to attention and, in an instant, sobered up. He was aghast and incredulous when the police arrived after they had been tipped off by a neighbor about some commotion inside the home of the old man.

Zacharis was summarily arrested and later convicted of a murder he did not commit. His so-called friends, he learned, had fled the village far from the arms of justice. Zacharis was committed to the *Agrotiki Filaki Kassandras*, the Kassandra Agricultural Jail on the remote northern Greek peninsula of Chalkidiki, hours away from home. He was sentenced to twelve years.

One hundred forty-four months, 4,380 days.

May 5, 1958.

It was while Zacharis was in jail that his baby was born at the General Hospital in the town of Arta. Vasilo delivered a sweet healthy baby girl. It is customary that a baby not be formally named until it can be baptized, which is traditional in the Greek Orthodox Church. The family would keep that tradition and would name the child after the paternal grandmother. She would be called Penelope, Popi, after Zacharis's mother, despite the animosity and cruelty of his father, and the family's disdainful attitude toward Vasilo.

When they were able, mother, daughter, and grandmother apprehensively returned to their village. The homecoming was painful because of the hushed, cruel whispering. They faced the shame, the stigma of a child born out of wedlock. And this was also a child, half of whom was a part of a more prominent family, and the other half to a family of lesser means. The Gyftokostas family had *perifaneia*, though. Pride. It gave them strength and was a quality that suited them well, especially now.

Giorgos Gyftokostas, a good and pious man, adored his daughter. He loved her more than any embarrassment he may have harbored about a grandchild born out of wedlock. He had an idea, an idea that would make his daughter's life easier. He decided to take her and his infant granddaughter to the jail where Zacharis was being held. It was the kind of jail where the inmates were required to toil in the fields, to be of some use while they served their time. It was painful for the Gyftokostas family to separate at a time when they needed each other most, but Constantina would take her cue from her husband and supported the decision. She took the small face of her granddaughter in her hands, looking intently, as if to memorize every tiny part of her.

Father and daughter traveled to the jail by bus, an arduous journey over difficult terrain even without an infant and fragile new mother. In an effort to wash away the stigma that branded the couple, Giorgos's plan was to appeal to the prison to let Zacharis see his baby and to ask someone, anyone, who was legally certified to do so, to perform a wedding ceremony. This way his daughter would have the husband she loved and his granddaughter would have parents, who were married.

This plan was not to materialize.

Giorgos begged. The three of them waited. Giorgos further explained their dilemma to the guards. "Please," he implored, "Let my daughter have the husband she deserves." They would check with the authorities. Again, they waited. The authorities returned but refused to relent. Giorgos pleaded. "Let him at least see his baby. Just for a moment. Please." They would not allow Zacharis to see his child, let alone hold her, kiss her, and to tell her that he would never forget her, that he would always be her father, and that he would come to her one day the minute he was free.

Crestfallen, they left the prison and journeyed to a shelter that cared for unwed mothers and their babies. It was on an island in Lake Pamvotida, near Ioannina, which was also populated with a cluster of monasteries. First by bus and then by small boat, they took the baby. Vasilo and her father decided to leave the child in the care of the shelter. They explained to the caregivers that they had to return to their village to think, to figure out what to do. It was complicated, they told the shelter. They explained that they were from a small, hostile village environment that did not want an unwed mother and a child born of a union that one prominent family did not want, under any circumstance, and would certainly shun. The caregivers at the shelter dispassionately listened, but agreed to help. They would keep and care for the baby until their return.

Vasilo and Giorgos, reluctantly and nervously, left the infant and headed back home by bus to their village. To Kastania. They quietly slipped back into town to take the temperature of what may have been happening and who might have been saying what. Things were hardly settled. The atmosphere remained tense and unpleasant. Zacharis's father did not want Vasilo in the village, and aggressively expressed his feelings in public as he worked at intimidating the entire Gyftokostas family.

The days crept by. Vasilo was distracted, anxious, and tense about her baby being left too long without her. Her father, also heartbroken, felt determined to do something about the situation, but he needed to think it through. In the end, he believed that his daughter, his family, were more important than any repercussions he might face in the village. Finally, he decided that nothing and no one would keep the baby from her mother, from her family, from her village. "She is our blood," Giorgos told his family. "We are going to bring her home to where she belongs," he said.

And with that the couple prepared to return to the shelter at Lake Pamvotida.

Constantina, Vasilo's mother, would stay back to tend to the fields and the children. She was the village seamstress and there was demand for her services. Soon, there would be another mouth to feed. They would need the money.

Father and daughter returned to the island shelter to retrieve the baby and make their way back home, accepting that the days ahead would be challenging. But when they arrived an attendant told them the baby was no longer there.

"What do you mean, no longer here," Vasilo quietly implored in disbelief, her voice growing small and strained.

"You signed the papers. You gave us permission to take the child, Miss Gyftokosta. Don't you remember?"

Vasilo began to panic. A pain welled up inside her chest as it stiffened. She felt her whole body tighten. She had signed no paper.

"Wait here," he said curtly.

The attendant returned with a non-descript paper, which he flailed around in the air at them, not letting her touch it, let alone see it. But she had signed for nothing, certainly not to relinquish her baby, not to anybody. She felt deceived. Duped. Stupid for trusting. She was certain they understood that she would be gone for a short time just to settle her affairs and return to take back her child.

As his own daughter was falling apart it was Giorgos now who questioned the attendant, desperately asking him to explain what had happened to his grandchild. He wanted to know at once where she had been taken. He got nowhere as the authorities at the shelter insisted that the mother had given her permission. They drew a small crowd as the tense back and forth continued. Giorgos's heart began to sink. He was poor and had no influence, no papers to prove anything. But if the baby was, in fact, gone what was the point of having any kind of written proof anyway, if they were claiming Vasilo had signed the child away?

Vasilo's mind raced as she doubted herself, angry for trusting anyone with her baby. Her heart swelled with emotion. Utterly distraught, slowly she began to unravel. A young, poor unwed mother, she had no power either and no means to help herself or her child. She knew in her heart, despite his efforts, that her father would be unable to alter their predicament. She had no official record of her baby, not even that she had been born to her.

Vasilo had only known her baby, held her, been able to love her for just 22 days.

Giorgos wrapped his grief-stricken daughter in his arms as she collapsed in his tight embrace. Reality began to sink in as Vasilo began to lose her composure and her mind. Her baby had been taken. The love of her life was behind bars, and the living evidence of their relationship had disappeared, vanished into thin air. Gone. Her baby was gone.

She wanted to die.

Giorgos pried his daughter away from the shelter and to a small boat that would shuttle them to shore. Crying and screaming as it pulled away from the island on Lake Pamvotida, Vasilo tried repeatedly to jump with the intention of drowning herself. Her father held her down as she thrashed about, inconsolable. Her cries of despair echoed across the lake to nothing and to no one there. Together they returned to Kastania, defeated and despondent.

It was sheer agony to have to place a phone call they had been dreading. From the one and only phone the village had, it was Giorgos, who called Zacharis to tell him about his daughter. It was too painful for Vasilo, who felt she had utterly failed him. Failed their child. Giorgos attempted to explain the trajectory of the story.

After Vasilo gave birth in Arta, they came to the prison to see Zacharis.

They were turned away.

They then took the child to a shelter as they figured out what to do.

They decided to go back to the shelter to bring the child home where she belonged, only to find that she had been given away or somehow lost or moved.

Had she fallen ill and was in a hospital somewhere?

Was she dead and had been buried?

"There is no trace of her," he said, with a sorrow that was overwhelming.

Zacharis was in shock. In disbelief. "How did this happen," he cried. "How could this have happened?" He did not blame Vasilo or Giorgos and, in fact, he was quite sympathetic despite his own pain. After all, he had made the same calculation, trusting someone to do what they said they would. His cunning, so-called friends were the reason he was locked away.

Zacharis was a quiet, proud, and modest man who so rarely showed emotion, but he sobbed on the phone, his head in his hands, wiping away the tears that wouldn't stop. "We will find a way to get to her," he said, attempting to choke back tears, but the truth was, he felt helpless facing so many years in prison ahead of him. Resigned, he knew he could do nothing to help them except to be there, strong and supportive of Vasilo from a distance, until he was released and could come home.

Vasilo decided then and there to don black clothing, the traditional color and expression of mourning. Her life would now lie motionless in spirit and space. She was broken and alone. She refused to leave the house. For six months she stayed in the family home focused on her sewing. Alone at night she wept for her baby, and for Zacharis. They exchanged letters, hundreds of them, which kept her centered and emotionally intact.

Separated by distance, walls, and bars, Vasilo worked to bolster the spirits of Zacharis through her own letters to him while he was locked away. She believed and fully trusted her own feelings. "*Ego eimai edo*," she told him. I am here. "*Tha eimai edo panta.*" I will always be here, she told him. Vasilo was determined to wait for her lover for as long as it would take. If she could not have him, she would want no other. She could never marry anyone else. And she meant it. It was a solemn promise she continually made because she had a deep and abiding faith in their relationship. She could love no other. Of that she was certain.

Zacharis would affirm his love for Vasilo, reassuring her

that everything in the end would be alright once they were together. In his own heart, deep and quiet, he knew that the promise of a life and future with Vasilo would be his ultimate salvation. His redemption. He would not express the extent of his anguish about their baby so as not to further upset Vasilo, who had chosen not only to wait for him, but to live a life cloistered, like a nun. She was alone, a quiet weaver.

She prayed.

Every day she prayed before her own *iconostasi*, a precious collection of icons, carefully placed on the wall in her room. She prayed before the forever-lit candle that bobbed in oil, cradled by a red glass vessel. Every day she whispered in Greek the *Pater Imon*, "Our Father, who art in heaven, hallowed be thy name." She would pray for the safety and happiness of her baby wherever she was. She would pray for her Zacharis, for him to remain strong during their separation. She prayed for her own strength as she endured the deep pain in her heart all day, every day, from the moment she opened her eyes in the morning until weary with emotion after the day was done, she closed them. She crossed herself three times. Each time, three fingers together. First at her forehead. Then to the mid-torso. From her right shoulder to the left. Flat palm pressed to her heart as if to seal in her silent hopes and wishes.

Amin. Amen.

From time to time people would tell Vasilo of babies they would see or hear about nearby, and that maybe one of them was hers. "This baby looked like the family," one said with certainty. In desperation someone would volunteer to search, to try to track down the tip where they had heard those babies had been seen, but any hope that was generated quickly fell to dust. Vasilo's heart sank deeper with each disappointment.

How could her heart, so completely broken, ever mend?

Twenty-two days was all she had to remember a child now gone. But she would hang on to that memory. The way she looked. The way she smelled, especially the sweetness of her baby's head. She would recall holding her to her chest, heart to heart. She thought about her child suckling at her breasts, watching her draw nourishment from her body to the baby's. It was that fleeting image of the baby feeding that held some hope for Vasilo that her child would be strong no matter what she faced, even if in the arms of another mother.

E aster had come.
It is the most significant, sacred holiday in all of Orthodoxy and a beautiful time of year. In small villages, like Kastania, the holiday is especially poignant and symbolic. Holy week is a period of prayer, fasting, and quiet reflection. Every day in church is meaningful as Greek Orthodox Christians recall and recount the final days of Christ. His final week on earth. His final meal. His crucifixion. His entombment and, finally, His ascension to heaven, from death to life everlasting, leading humanity out of the darkness and into the light by following Him.

For days before, villagers prepare for the resurrection by baking bread, marinating a baby lamb to break the fast, and dying red eggs to symbolize Christ's blood that was shed for them. It is the *Anastasi* service (at midnight on Saturday) that is the most moving and the most dramatic, which re-enacts the moment when Christ ascends to the heavens in a brilliant burst of light and hope. The church is in darkness when the priest talks about how Satan is defeated by the triumph of Christ over death as he is returned to His Father. One light from one candle lights the next. And another lights another until the entire church is re-awakened, bathed in light, incense wafting through the dank, stale air.

Vasilo's father and mother begged her, as they had every Easter since the baby disappeared, to come to church for the *Anastasi* service. "It will do you good, my child," her father said. "*Ela mazi mas.*" Come with us. For six years, as she had every year, Vasilo refused and would stay home, prepare the table, and wait until after midnight to greet her family. They would return sheltering lit candles from the night air, and take the flickering light to every room in the small house, marking each space for a year of good fortune and blessings ahead. Then they would eat together, breaking a 40-day fast.

It was nearing midnight when Vasilo needed to use the loo, which was an outdoor privy some distance from the house. As she was leaving it to return to the main house, she could not ignore a bright light gleaming from the mountainside across from Kastania. It hovered there; a burst, a spectacular ball of light. She froze in place as it began to move across the valley and toward her. She was terrified, but in awe of it. Her feelings caught up to her as she ran inside, finding herself in front of the icons and forever-lit candle where a calm began to melt over her. She thought for a minute and accepted the light as a sign from the *Panayia* herself, the mother of Christ, as she simultaneously heard from a distance, loud and clear from the church, "*Christos Anesti*," Christ is risen! And the villagers responded in unison, "*Alithos Anesti*," Truly he has risen! Vasilo decided in that moment that she would also emerge from her seclusion, from her own tomb.

Vasilo believed she had received a divine message. It was a sign that something good was bound to happen, and that gave her some comfort.

Dena Polites loved to Greek dance!

Raised in Columbus, Ohio, the only child of a wealthy business owner and a homemaker, she was a groupie. She and her friends would follow the band and music of Takis and the Grecian Keys. They played at weddings, baptisms, and other Greek celebrations in and around Columbus. Dena never needed an excuse to go to a Greek dance.

Her cousin Kathy remembered how "beautifully" and "soulfully" Dena would take the floor. "There could be a hundred people on that dance floor, but all eyes were always on Dena," said Kathy. "She was graceful and could feel the music like no one else. She was so good at it that people would cede the front of the line to Dena so that they could watch her captivate the room, and inspire them to feel what she did when she was dancing."

This was especially true when she danced the *tsamiko*, which was her favorite. The *tsamiko* was once a dance only for men, but that changed over the years. Dena was made for the *tsamiko*, a dance in which the leader is the one singular attraction.

Pretty, petite, and blond, Dena had oval-shaped, sparkling hazel eyes that changed color with the light or the clothing she wore. She had an effervescent personality. She enjoyed socializing with her friends and so would often accompany her parents, prominent Ohio Greeks, Nick and Amelia, to an annual reunion of people from or near Tsintzina, which is a small village near the legendary Sparta in the Peloponnese region of Greece where the family was from. The group would gather in Jamestown, New York every year at the end of July for a convention. For the Greek diaspora, this was one of the oldest reunions of its kind in the United States.

It was during a meeting of the Tsintzinians in 1976, and across a crowded dance floor, when young Christos Poulias, a Greek boy from Ithaca, New York first laid eyes on Dena.

It was lust at first sight.

He was instantly drawn to her. Cautious and respectful of the event and the elders in attendance, he subtly tried to get Dena's attention. He flirted with her. They talked a bit. He watched her dance. He was captivated by her style of dancing and passion on the dance floor just like everyone else. This chance encounter would serve as a prelude to the future, but this particular meeting served only as a tantalizing appetizer. For Christos.

Dena had been dating another Greek guy from Columbus, whom she very much liked. And she was going to Greece on vacation, a place where more memories would be created in the romantic, intoxicating land of sun, blue, white-cubed houses, and the wine-dark sea.

"Why don't you pack me in your suitcase," Christos sweetly quipped. She thought the comment was cute, but this would not particularly draw her in any way to Christos. She liked his mustache, his Greek accent. It was cute the way his lip twitched a bit when he spoke. But he was forgotten and the encounter was not memorable, at least not for Dena.

In 1980, Christos returned to a reunion of Tsintzinians in Jamestown specifically to see Dena. It was one of the rare years she did not attend. She had decided, instead, to go to a choir convention in Toronto. But Christos ran into Dena's father and told him he was disappointed to learn he would not see his daughter. They talked for a bit and Christos made a good impression on Nick. They discussed the national convention the following month of the powerful, respected Greek organization called the AHEPA (American Hellenic Educational Progressive Association), created to promote Hellenic ideals, including values such as education, philanthropy, civic responsibility, family, and service through volunteerism.

The Polites family, prominent, involved, big-donor members had planned to attend. Christos decided to be there as well. He offered to extend his employee discount at the Hilton Hotel in Washington because he worked at the Hilton in New York City. This pleased Nick Polites, who very much wanted his daughter to meet this unassuming, nice-looking Greek boy from Ithaca, New York and to "give him a try."

Christos spoke no English when he came to America from Greece as a 13-year-old with his brother, John, and parents, Costas and Maria Poulias. Maria was from the village of *Goritsa*, near Sparta. Costas was from *Kalyvia Sohas*, also near Sparta, in the Peloponnese. Working-class people, they settled in Ithaca, New York.

Costas worked three jobs for a couple of Greek-owned restaurants and as a janitor in a school. Maria was a seamstress for the drama department at Ithaca College, which enabled Christos to attend as a student. John went to SUNY

Plattsburgh in upstate New York. They were a good, humble, down-to-earth family. They loved to entertain, but did not stand on ceremony. Their home reflected the epitome of *filoxenia*, the hospitality for which Greeks are famous, and which extends even to strangers.

Maria was the consummate hostess, who exemplified this tradition. The house was warm and welcoming, people in and out, always there for coffee and sweets or for a meal, which was never too much to provide, even at a moment's notice.

Christos had memorable teenage and college years in Ithaca. He graduated from the prestigious liberal arts school and got a job in sales for the Hilton Hotel in Manhattan. He lived and commuted to work from the nearby Greek enclave of Astoria, Queens.

There was something in Christos that Nick Polites wanted for his daughter, Dena. He was charming and polite. A gentleman. And Nick liked that he was open and direct about liking and wanting to get to know his daughter. Christos knew he was also courting Nick so that he could get closer to his daughter. So that father would trust a young suitor with his daughter. Winning the affection of Dena would later be her own salvation. It would also change the dynamics between father and son-in-law and father and son-in-law's family.

Nick began to encourage Dena to meet Christos, telling her of his good qualities. "He's a good boy from a nice family," Nick told his daughter. "I checked him out." Dena remained uninterested, but her father persisted as they traveled, against her will, to Washington, D.C. for the AHEPA National Convention.

The Polites family arrived, got settled in their rooms, and decided to take a walk through the lobby to see who of their friends might have already arrived. As the elevator eased to the ground floor and with the sound of a ping, the doors silently slid open, and there waiting in the lobby to get on, was Christos Poulias. He was startled, but delighted to run into Dena and her parents.

Serendipity.

They exchanged pleasantries and Christos invited Dena then and there to the pool area for a drink. Nick was pleased that his daughter needed no prodding to accept the invitation as they parted company for the remainder of the evening. Dena would not defy her father. He was intimidating and always pushed for what he wanted, typically, until Dena relented. "I was always afraid of him," Dena remembers. But this would be a rare moment in her life when she was unusually grateful for her father's pressure and influence.

At the pool, Christos reminded Dena of Jamestown, New York those years ago when they had first met and spoken briefly at a dance. She didn't remember him at all until he asked her, "Do you remember a guy asking you if you could pack him in your suitcase... when you were going to Greece?" That clicked. "That was YOU," Dena asked. "That was me."

The drink by the pool lasted for two hours. Christos did most of the talking about who he was, where he came from, his parents, his dreams, his aspirations, his goals. Dena began to focus on this charming young Greek and felt at ease and engaged in what he had to say. She was interested in his life and found him as open and as warm as her father had. They decided to skip all of the AHEPA festivities that night, and there were many. Instead, they hailed a taxi to Georgetown where they spent another three hours over dinner talking at the Public House, a popular, trendy eatery.

The next day the couple decided to visit the world-famous Washington, D.C. National Zoo to see the new pandas that had ceremoniously arrived from China. Later, as luck would have it, they hailed the same cab driver they had ridden with the night before. They asked to go to the same restaurant in hopes of repeating the connection they had established during the previous evening.

Kismet.

The magic and the spark were still there and pulsed, glowing even brighter. Again, for hours they talked, but this time it was Dena who did most of it. She talked about her life, her parents. She shared incidental information. She had been named for her father's mother, Constantina. Dena for short. And she shared consequential information. When she was seven years old, she learned that she was adopted. It was upsetting, confusing to be told at age seven, that the parents you had known, did not give birth to you. She told Christos all that she knew, and there wasn't much.

Her biological mother had died during childbirth.

Her father was unknown to anyone.

She had been left—she didn't know how or when or

with whom— in an orphanage somewhere in Sparta.

It was there where her adoptive family had heard there was a baby, who needed a home.

She was 14 months old when she was transported by a woman to her new family.

Nick and Amelia Polites met their new baby in New York City and traveled with her to Columbus, Ohio, bringing her into their lives.

That is all she knew. That is all she was told, she said to Christos. She did not disclose, however, that she was terrified to ask her adoptive parents for any more information about her early life.

By day, every day, Zacharis worked the fields. In a way, the hard labor was welcome in order to divert his mind and feelings. In the silence of the night, alone in his cell, he would gaze out from the fortified window at the fields and mountains in the distance. They changed color with the rise and setting of the sun each day. That is the picture of freedom, he thought.

He pondered what better days might look like. He expressed silent gratitude for his life and his love for Vasilo. He felt no bitterness. He was not angry at anyone, except maybe himself. He was resigned, keeping a calendar, and marking the days as the 48 seasons of confinement passed.

He thought about his *clarino* and recalled the village music he used to play, hearing every note in his head as he visualized the way his fingers deftly moved over the tone holes, punctuating the music where the emphasis belonged with the padded keys of his instrument.

Zacharis consciously worked at more positive thoughts and did not necessarily want to dwell on the past, but he had all the time in the world to do so. Twelve years, 144 months, and 4,380 days. And so, sometimes he did.

Dwell.

Winters were particularly hard in the north of the country. It seemed even more cold. It seemed even more remote. The darkness of the season would entice worry. And regret. Why had he gotten involved in a petty crime that ended up in a murder charge? Why had he had anything to do with those so-called friends, who deserted him in the end? Why didn't he fight harder to defend his innocence?

He blamed his behavior on despair and his desire to break free from his father's toxic grasp on his life. He so desperately wanted his father to understand that he wanted Vasilo as much as she wanted him, and that she was wonderful. His father had so harshly judged her, Zacharis thought, and he hated the way his own family disparaged the Gyftokostas family, their attitude toward them, treating them as inferiors, and looking down on them when they all came from the same small, poor village. Yes, some had a little more than others, but they were all fellow Kastanians, just the same.

Then there was the guilt. The pain that he had caused, the heartache, and deep sadness about the old man, who had lost his life. What was any of it for?

There was little to nothing he could do to help Vasilo because of his own irresponsible decisions. He couldn't support her through the birth of their child, knowing she would have a difficult time without the love of both families coming together to make a home. He worried about who was taking care of her. At least he trusted the love of her family and that they would be there for her. Vasilo's father was so devoted, so loving, he thought. That was the kind of father he wanted to be, if ever he had the chance again.

To moro. The baby. *His* baby.

Alone with his thoughts, he worried and wondered all night, every night about his child. Where was she? Who was caring for her? Was she healthy? Was she even alive? His thoughts were tortured, persistent, tangled, as he stared at the four walls, sometimes glancing at the sky and moon above through the small window of his cell. He should be with Vasilo, he thought, by her side, loving her, and sharing, enduring together the loss of their first born.

Zacharis prayed. Without any icons, without any forever-lit candle, he looked to the stars in the heavens above and he prayed.

His heart hurt. Could a heart so completely broken ever mend?

Zacharis's life was not his own, but he fought the surrender of his mind, which could be a prison, too. He may have felt hopeless and powerless about the reality of a cruel, controlling father, but his love for Vasilo not only endured, but grew in all those days and months and years. His *clarino* had been taken from him, and even if he had it with him, he wouldn't be allowed to play it, nor would he be in any mood to do so. It was through his music that the quiet man-of-few-words, Zacharis, had expressed himself. Now he needed a different way, another way. He channeled his thoughts and feelings through letters.

Letters.

Over a hundred of them in the years that Zacharis was away. In those letters, he would write the words he could never find. His words, in cadence and description, were the music he now made in the absence of his instrument. He loved Vasilo more than he ever had. He reassured her that he would be there for her once he got out of prison. He told her not to worry. "You are my only love," he wrote. "We will be together." His letters to her were the only things that helped him to maintain his own sanity.

Vasilo loved his respect for her in those letters; his care, his sensitivity and his strength. Zacharis had also been writing to her sister, Stamatia, encouraging her to help keep Vasilo strong and to keep her spirits up. He was charming and warm, and he worked hard at instilling a confidence in Vasilo that they would never abandon their love for each other. They both needed all the strength they could muster after Vasilo and her father had to confess to Zacharis that their baby had vanished, and that she was the one who had trusted those promising to care for her. Zacharis remained steadfast, not angry, just bereft. And lonely. Longing to be at home with the woman he loved.

The years passed.

Zacharis had trained his mind and emotions to live with, to fully accept his reality and the slow passage of time.

It was not until 1970 when Zacharis unceremoniously walked out of prison on his own and into the glaring light of day. Alone, he found a bus home to Kastania. Waiting for him were Vasilo and her family, who warmly greeted him and embraced him; they were grateful for his return to her and to his home.

From his own family it was a different story. His father remained obstinate as were his mother and sisters. They refused to warm to Vasilo. They refused to even try. He told his family that his love for Vasilo had not diminished, but instead had grown. He had every intention of marrying her, he said. They had created a child together and they had lost her. He told his parents they had waited faithfully and patiently for each other through twelve years of an excruciating separation. If they could make it this far still so much in love, the union was meant to be.

Giorgos's ire toward the couple, especially toward Vasilo, had also not diminished in those dozen years. "She is not good enough for you," he told his son. "She is beneath you, beneath our family. If you insist on marrying her you are not my son! From me, you will get no money, no house, no help, no anything." Zacharis was undeterred. But his father was true to his word.

Indeed, Zacharis got nothing.

The couple was resilient, though. Quietly they planned. Vasilo was an excellent seamstress and would save her money as she serviced the villagers who needed clothes mended, dresses and trousers created and fitted. An uncle of Vasilo promised to help the couple build a home, and so he did with Zacharis. For three years, the couple pulled together the threads of a life that would sustain them, with or without the support of the Papazacharis family. They had each other and they had a loving Gyftokostas family by their side.

Three years later, in 1973, they wed. It was a small quiet ceremony of some 30 people in the village church. Zacharis's father, Giorgos, *did* decide to attend, not because he necessarily wanted to, but *"yia ta matia,"* for the eyes of others because he would be shamed by other villagers for refusing to come to the wedding of his own son. His only son. He was not at all happy about it, but at least he and his family were present to witness the cementing of an enduring love.

After the ceremony, there was a dinner on the first floor of their small home. Afterwards, the chairs and tables were cleared to the side of the room. Someone found a radio and tuned in a scratchy, distant station that played Greek music. They danced. Vasilo danced for Zacharis like she used to. They danced together as man and wife. But there would be no traditional song and dance for the bride, *"oraia pou einai i nifi mas,"* how beautiful is our bride. While joyous for the couple, the celebration was muted.

There was someone missing. Their baby. She was always at the back of their minds and in their hearts, despite their relief and happiness about their own survival. They were complete in their love, but their family was not, and would never be. They were forced to just live with it and to make a new life, loving her always from afar, and hoping that in some place, somewhere, someone was caring for her, loving her, and making her happy.

The years passed slowly as they often do in remote mountain villages, but in 1974 their hearts were filled by the birth of a son, named Giorgos, George, after both grandfathers. Nineteen months later, in 1976, the couple had a daughter whom they named Penelope, Popi, for short, after Zacharis's mother, as was customary.

Dena tried not to give much thought to her status as an adoptee. She did not dwell on the adoption and had asked very few questions over the years. It was rendered a footnote in her privileged life; she was afraid to pry into the circumstances of her birth. She did not want to upset her father, who may have taken offense by regarding her curiosity as ingratitude. Those feelings were kept deeply buried, and so in the telling of her own story, what little she knew, it held not much importance.

In turn, it held little significance for Christos. He took his cue from her. She would also privately hold her painful experience of growing up in the volatile Polites household—

vulnerabilities that were hard to talk about with anyone unless they had witnessed it themselves. Unless they were part of the family. And what would Christos think? She did not want to scare him off now that she had come to like him so much.

Their second date ended very late. Outside the hotel, they kissed and kissed again, and told each other they didn't want to leave. Christos would take a bus back to Queens the next morning. Dena would return to Columbus with her parents, who were delighted that the match was beginning to take.

The encounter began a long-distance relationship, which included lingering, lengthy phone calls and weekend trips back and forth between New York and Columbus. Christos would stay at a friend's home in Columbus while visiting Dena. Dena would lie to her parents saying she was staying with friends while visiting Christos in Queens, but stayed with him. "Nice Greek girls" had reputations to protect and their parents made sure, as much as they could, that they remained chaste. The couple certainly could not, and never would, consider staying at the homes of each other's parents. It just wasn't done. It wasn't proper. And the parents would not have allowed it anyway.

Dena and Christos did fall deeply in love, but Dena would also admit that she needed to get out of the house for good. A marriage would ultimately take care of that. With Christos she felt safe. He empowered her. He adored her. He was entirely the opposite of her own father. And so, in February 1981, the couple were engaged. It wasn't until the engagement that Christos was allowed to stay with Dena and her parents, but only until he found his own apartment. In July of the same year, they were married with several hundred friends and relatives in attendance at a traditional Greek wedding celebration, a lavish affair, which began at the Annunciation Greek Orthodox Church in Columbus, Ohio.

The festivities surrounding the nuptials were not without drama, pain, and embarrassment. Before the wedding there was to be a party at the Polites home, a rehearsal dinner, and a bachelor party for the groom and his friends. Relatives from Ithaca, New York had driven eight hours to be there for the groom. But suddenly, Nick Polites put out the word that he wanted no one from the groom's side at any of it. They simply were not welcome. The couple was hurt and Christos was angry. Dena was embarrassed, but froze, unable to do anything about it in the moment. It was her wedding and her father was footing the bill. But her father's behavior stung. Christos ended up throwing himself a party at the hotel where his friends and family were staying.

Things got worse on the day of the wedding. Dena's priest, Father Anthony Sarris, was to officiate and the couple decided that a dear friend of theirs, also a priest, Father Seraphim Poulos, whom they had both known from the gathering of the Tsintzinians every year in Jamestown, New York, would also join in the sacrament. He, too, had driven for hours to be there to celebrate the couple. To bless the couple. To be there for his friends, who had specifically requested his presence and participation. But this was also not to be.

Nick Polites forbade the priest access to the ceremony. He would not allow it, and sent him away. Father Seraphim was upset and desperate to talk to Christos. When he found him moments before he was to meet his bride at the altar, he said, "Your future father-in-law does not want me around. I am leaving." Chris was stunned and also paralyzed to do anything about it. It was his wedding day, a day to be one of the happiest in his life. His impulse was to focus on Dena, not this. But the swirling, tangled events that surrounded him were difficult to dismiss. "Chris," the priest said, with intensity, anguish, and concern, "If you can get out of this situation, get out. Get out now. The family is not good. This is not good." With that he was gone, leaving Chris with an ache in his heart and a pit in his stomach.

Despite this let down, this duality of feelings and emotions, which clashed with a moment in time to be cherished, the sacrament of marriage happened as it has for millennia in the Orthodox Church. And it was happy. The couple took their first steps as one, joined by *stefana*, white, delicate "crowns," attached one to the other by a single white ribbon. They circled a small table three times in front of the altar. Their hands, joined together, were covered by one hand of the priest, an impressive gilded Bible cradled against his chest with the other. He led them around and around, singing hymns of gratitude to God, and expressions of joy for the couple. This was the ancient Dance of Isaiah.

Dena would particularly remember this solemn dance, the first steps with her new husband, her best friend, a person whom she would refer to as her soulmate, her rock, her protector. She now belonged to him. With him. The bond to her parents, to her father, was broken, and she was now cleaved to her husband, a man who would take her from the unhappy home she grew up in to create a home, a happy home, of their own. Three hundred people, mostly Nick's friends and family, were at the wedding. Just two tables were reserved for the family and friends of the groom.

But they danced. They all danced and the *nifi*, the bride, took her place at the front of the line— an age-old tradition, so that she could be the center of attention, to honor her, adore her. Dena loved to dance and, as always, all eyes were on her, like never before. On this day she danced for the first time, a married woman.

Dena's *prika*, her dowry, her wedding gift, was a health food store that her parents gave to the couple. It was not necessarily what the couple wanted or was interested in, but it would put them into a business of their own. It was a means of income and support. Nick, Dena's father, was never to be argued with. He was domineering and controlling. It was during these first years of marriage, before the couple would have children of their own, when Christos learned more about his wife's early years, growing up with a man who was volatile and unpredictable.

Nick Polites was an imposing figure, had a dark disposition, disagreeable and critical, with a personality that was unattractive. It repelled people. Bright spots were always hard to find. He easily and often disrupted family gatherings, dinners, and outings with an explosive temper as he dominated conversations and bullied those around him to do things his way. Arguments were to be expected. They were loud and persisted. He always perseverated on and on.

As a child, Dena remembers repeatedly hiding in the night underneath a night table that was covered with a floor length cloth. She would sleep walk as a child and admits that some memories may be obscured, too painful, too deep to recall with any clarity. Some things do not and just cannot come to the surface. That world was opaque and dark. It needed to be carefully navigated and negotiated. It was painful. It hurt to be Nick's child, especially his only child, with no one else at home to confide in.

A cousin also remembers Nick's insensitivity, his disregard for the feelings of others. Kathy, the closest person to a sibling Dena would have, recalls playing with her cousin inside the Polites house as they gazed out a picture window in the living room. The children were giggling as young girls do, bouncing on the sofa when they spotted a rabbit that had hopped to the center of the lawn. It stopped and stood up on its hind legs sniffing the air at nothing in particular, contemplating what to do next. The girls were delighted with the tiny creature, admiring it, when suddenly an arrow with the sharp trajectory of a well-thrown javelin came from nowhere and was driven into the tiny chest of the rabbit. It fell as Nick emerged with a bow. He was a hunter and this child's delight was little more than prey. The girls were inconsolable. He laughed and mocked their tears.

Kathy's mother, Sophia, and Dena's mother, Amelia, were sisters. It was no secret in the family that Nick was a difficult man. He dominated discussions and was quick to anger. He was aggressive and abusive to his wife and young daughter. Life was as he saw it. As he wanted it. Amelia and Dena were too intimidated, too frightened to challenge him. They took it, wanting to just keep the peace, avoiding an eruption, and the barrage of insults and accusations that would inevitably follow. Most of the family took it, too, seemingly, to shield and protect Amelia from any more pain and animosity in her home. They were fearful for her safety, and so for her sake, avoided antagonizing Nick further. The Polites home was continually punctuated with emotional and physical abuse. Nick would hit Amelia. He hit Dena.

Sophia was Amelia's younger sister. She was an artist, a

painter, and a skilled potter. Her non-Greek husband, Bill, was a professor in music history and taught the French horn at the University of Boulder. They had left Ohio for Colorado in 1965 when cousins Kathy and Dena were eight years old. Bill and Sophia had returned back to Ohio after a few years to take a trip with Nick and Amelia. The sisters wanted to see each other. It had been too long.

Nick owned an RV and decided that the foursome would take a drive through New England to bask in the iconic fall foliage made famous in that part of the country. Nick was the self-anointed only one allowed to drive, and he would decide when and where they stopped along the way. Bill had always wanted to visit The Mount, the home of American author, Edith Wharton, in quaint, charming Lenox, Massachusetts, in the heart of the Berkshires. Bill was a poet, a writer, and man of letters beyond his teaching. This diversion during their journey would have pleased him greatly and made for a happy traveler. But Nick, in characteristic fashion, ignored the request and drove right past.

The trip was not a shared experience. It was Nick's experience. He merely took a captive group along. The journey turned out to be terrifically unpleasant, but the thought of how Amelia might later pay for any mutiny, was more important than any confrontation. Sophia and Bill loved their sister and sister-in-law enough to anticipate the irrational behavior of fragile Nick, to understand delicate boundaries and identify where the vulnerabilities lay. They were angry, but kept quiet. And they were resolved never again to repeat traveling with them.

Amelia and Sophia had come from the same Koumantarakis home, but the women were so different in their choice of men. Amelia, a secretary and housewife, had chosen a volatile partner, domineering, cruel, and often frightening. It was as if Nick neither enjoyed nor was interested in being a husband or a father. Nick had lost his mother at a very young age and never recovered from that loss. He was perpetually angry.

Sophia was an artist and housewife. She had chosen a gentle musician and teacher, who was a devoted husband and loving father. Bill's ancestors could be traced as far back as the Mayflower. They were good Methodists and were from English, Irish, and Scottish stock. Theirs was a happy home.

But also, the difference here was that one was Greek, the other was not. Many Greeks of that era both tolerated and perpetuated the patriarchy. Life was often centered around the male and they were ascribed certain properties and privileges at birth, by their families with particular allowances that were rarely, if ever, challenged.

Men were adored. Men were cherished. Women were precious, but marginalized and were required to please the men in their life, whether it be their fathers or brothers or uncles. They were raised and expected to be good wives and mothers. Attractive to the men in their lives. This was not up for question or argument. Women acquiesced and had two central purposes in life.

One was to marry a Greek man, one who was suitable and could provide. The other was to have children. Women's desires, their wants and needs were simply unimportant. These gender roles were ingrained at an early age. Women had to be desirable, proper, good Greek girls, and it often meant surrender because what men said and what they wanted was the order of the day. Period. Women's own dreams often were not entertained, let alone realized.

This was where Amelia found herself with her own husband. She had chosen a man of her own culture and religion. All through the 1960's, a significant sector of the Greek-American culture was still clannish, incestuous, and imposing. Her sister, Sophia, had broken out, having chosen a husband from another culture outside of the bubble.

Why did Amelia stay? Poor self-esteem may have been part of it. Maybe she felt she was not worthy of a better man. It was clear she felt threatened and was fearful. She kept the peace because, otherwise, she ran the risk of being hit. How could she possibly make it on her own with a child? Could she count on her own family to be there as a resource for protection? Were she to have left her husband, would she be stigmatized? Maybe she thought that together they had money. They were, at least, secure. And maybe most important of all, what would other people, other Greek people, think? Divorce was shameful, a failure, and not common in their culture.

Abuse in Greek homes is simply not discussed. It is taboo. Domestic abuse exists, of course, as it does in many cultures, but the problem is closeted, deeply buried within family structures. Problems cannot get better unless and until they are cleansed in the light of day, but the airing of such issues in Greek homes was just too much.

Greeks have a universal image to protect and uphold. They are full of life and love and they are family-centered. Children are cherished and marriages celebrated. They have *kefi,* they love dancing. They are larger than life. The self-portrayal of exuberant, loving Greeks and the reality of domestic abuse are incongruous. It just doesn't work. It makes no sense. It cannot be. And so, there was silence and hurt and violence. Sometimes there was unimaginable behavior. Asking for help, getting help, airing grievances, and bringing to light deeply buried family problems is a stigma. There would be judgment and repercussions.

Amelia and Nick Polites were wealthy, influential Greeks in Columbus, Ohio. They had an image to uphold and Amelia Polites was painfully aware of her place and of her awful predicament. She was a Greek wife and mother of a certain time. She needed to behave, to keep her mouth shut, and to follow the will of her husband, even if it meant hurting her child.

Nick Polites perhaps thought that his son-in-law would treat women as he did his own wife, which would make his own behavior look acceptable. But Christos, while coming from Greek parents himself, represented a new, younger generation of Greek men. And his own parents were different. They were respectful of each other and had raised both of their boys to treat women the same way. Christos Poulias was nothing like Nick Polites. And that was a problem that grew over time.

At first, Nick loved Dena's new husband and at every turn took credit for the marriage. He believed that gave him license to direct the couple's plans for the future, navigate their dreams, and impose his own desires on them. He constantly tried to tell them how to run the health food store, which he had given the couple as a wedding gift. It was a high price to pay for his support.

The couple later sold the store and moved to Worcester, Massachusetts. They needed to get away from the pressure of a father who wanted control of a marriage that could not breathe free. They considered buying a pizza place, but ultimately decided against it. The couple contemplated working in real estate. Maybe renovating homes and flipping them. Nothing was of much appeal. Ultimately, each settled on working in offices doing jobs that held little significance or meaning. Dena's mother, Amelia, was supportive of their efforts, a new couple trying to find their own way. Nick, though, was an "I-told-you-so" kind of guy. "If you had listened to me, you wouldn't be making these crazy mistakes, stabbing around in the dark," he would say.

Despite the challenge of finding work and creating a life together, one of the couple's greatest joys were Christos's parents, who had come to visit for a few months from New York. They would shuttle back and forth between the homes of their sons. John, Christos's older brother and his wife, Linda, also lived in Worcester. Dena would come to know her in-laws more intimately. Their warmth. Their love. Their care. Their respect for her. She gained their appreciation for loving their son so completely. Dena was struck by the difference in these parents and her own. But she understood her mother's predicament. Or tried to. It was her father, Nick, who was the outlier, the narcissist, and master manipulator.

Jealousy began to bake in.

Nick was eaten up inside about his daughter growing closer to Christos's parents, their constant visiting, and their growing influence. He began to communicate with Maria, Christos's mother, even crying to her about how they missed their daughter, their only child. He told her of a potential business opportunity back in Columbus that would be good for the couple. "It will be very good for your son's future," he told the sympathetic Maria. "They could be set for life," Nick pressed. "Help me," he insisted, "Convince them to come back home." Over time he worked over the sympathetic Maria.

Maria admitted she felt sorry for Nick and Amelia and began to encourage her son and Dena to seriously think about the offer, made sweeter by Nick saying he would help them—help them financially. It was the father of a boy the Polites baptized, who had made the offer to finance the purchase of a business. Behind the scenes he was being encouraged, prodded by Nick, to make the offer, promising to provide the down payment for the couple.

It was against her better judgement, but the dutiful Greek daughter, the only child of a wealthy, influential businessman, and her supportive husband, returned home to Columbus. They were the new owners of Niki's Restaurant and Deli. They moved into Dena's childhood home with her parents so that they could gain some financial traction.

That decision was fraught with pot-holes and problems, though. They were subject to the bullying of Nick. And no money, no help, no down payment ever came for the business. When Dena reminded him about the money, his promise, Nick's response was that he never made such an offer. The couple felt betrayed, angry, and worried, but Nikitas Halkias, a good and dear friend, said not to worry about money. He would finance them. "Pay me monthly. Pay what you can. I don't want you to worry," he told them.

Christos's relationship with his father-in-law began to sour. He realized he had been coerced into coming back. It had been a set up. The two couples co-existed in the same house, but there was no warmth. They had little to do with one another.

Christos and Dena put their efforts into their marriage and the new business, which slowly morphed into what they knew best, Greek food. They added gyro sandwiches and favorites such as *pastitsio*, Greek lasagna, and *moussaka*, a variation of *pastitsio* that is eggplant-based.

It was a good business and it became successful. But they lived with Dena's parents and that was a strain. It also evoked sad memories of being a child, growing up at home with her father, a father she so desperately wanted acceptance and affection from, and to be close to. But Nick was not a warm man. He was abrupt and irascible. He often imposed it on the couple. And he was cruel.

In fact, he and Amelia would frequently come to the deli where Nick made a habit of telling the couple what needed to be done, what could be done better. Why this? Why that? The deli was challenging enough without additional pressure and unwanted advice. It was thriving. And sometimes it became chaotic when it was busy. There was no room for any additional drama. Christos began to have little patience for Nick's constant prying and loud opinions. He felt bullied.

One day Nick's godson, 10-year-old Yiannis, had come to the store when Nick and Amelia also happened to be there. The child's father, Nikitas Halkias, who had helped Dena and Christos afford the deli they now owned, was their *koumbaro*, someone who holds special significance, joined to a Greek family through a religious ceremony like a baptism, in this case. He had a restaurant across the street and his son visited Christos and Dena often.

Yiannis was a rambunctious boy and was running up and down, back and forth in the store just being a kid. Chris didn't necessarily mind, but Nick was annoyed. Irritated to the point of combustion. He managed to catch the child by the scruff of his neck, took him by the shoulders, and violently shook him. He hit him, tossing him to the floor. "You little shit. Stop it. Son of a bitch, this is a store. You stop running." Furious, Christos immediately stepped in. This was too much. Too far. "Get out. Don't you ever do that again. He's a kid. You don't touch a child like that. Get. Out."

Dena watched this scene unfold and it was painfully familiar. A father who was not a father. Who was unable. Incapable. She remembered. She held memories she wished she could forget, hoping they would not be awakened, that the dust would just settle on them, that they would remain dormant in the faded archives of her mind. But they surfaced. They emerged just the same.

There was something, something from her teenage years. A high school prom. A date. An opportunity to go out and have fun with her friends. It was one of those times that marks an important chapter in a young life. A rite of passage. Her father had granted his permission for her to attend the prom, but insisted she be home by 11. "Come on," she implored her father. "**Eleven**?" Alright, he said, relenting. "Midnight." At least it was something. One more hour. As all teenagers do, though, she pushed it, and came home at 1:30 am.

Nick was waiting.

He followed her into her bedroom, slammed the door, and began the all too familiar harangue. "Why do you treat me like this? Why do you do this?" He was yelling, his voice rising in volume, his face contorting, turning red. Dena felt his anger. His hatred. Was it for her?

"I have given you everything. EVERYTHING. And you have no respect." Dena began to cry. He walked toward her, came for her until she was backed up to the bed where she fell backward. He was straddling her now, hands wrapped around her throat. Her eyes closed tight, tears squeezing out from the corners. She held her breath so she wouldn't have to gasp for it.

"You are not my blood," he said with coldness and a particular emotional distance, as if she was a stranger. He abruptly released his hand from her throat. Standing up now, he began a frantic search for a suitcase and he began packing her things, randomly throwing in one thing after another. "Get out. I want you out. You are not. My. Blood." Dena did leave that night, walking down the street with her suitcase in the darkness, but he called her back eventually. Maybe it was Amelia, who implored her husband to stop what he was doing. But you can't take back words when they leave you.

Not. My. Blood.

It was a refrain that Dena would hear over and over again her entire life, especially in the heat of an argument. If she were not his; not his daughter; not his blood, then he could perhaps make better sense of the relationship he had with her in his own perverse mind. Perhaps it was to separate. Perhaps it somehow gave him permission to abuse her, to do unspeakable things a biological father would not, could never do.

Secrets.

They are inherently dark. They are inherently destructive. They are kept to the detriment of all involved, except to the perpetrator of such secrets, the keeper of such secrets. With secrets one cannot grow. One cannot heal. One cannot understand one's life or place in the world under the weight and veil of secrets. Compounding the pain of secrets, at least in this case, further dramatized the stigma of adoption.

Adopted.

It is an interesting state of being. You are not *of* your

adoptive parents, but you *become* theirs, certainly in a legal sense. Where the grace, where the magic flourishes is in the attitude of the parents, who take you from wherever you were, create a home for you, love you, and raise you as their very own. You don't grow under your adoptive mother's heart. You grow in it. For an adoptee to ever hear the words, even in anger, that you are not really a child of the parents raising you, reinforces an adoptee's own insecurities and vulnerabilities. It keeps them off balance. They are always "the other one." They are continually reminded of their difference. It feels, sometimes, like they belong to no one.

And it is soul-crushing.

From Amelia, Dena admits that she did feel love. She felt that Amelia regarded her as her own child. But Amelia had failed to protect Dena from her father. She was a submissive wife, a woman of her time, and also frightened of her husband. Whatever happened in the house, just happened.

Secrets.

Affection between mother and daughter was forced into temperance and co-existed with the dark clouds always in the distance that in an instant could erupt into an unpredictable violent storm, which was the brutality of Nick's attitude. It was an attitude that wielded pain and imposed control. The order of the day for Dena was survival, to avoid punishment, and Nick's wrath. At times, she wanted to be invisible.

More often than not, the holidays were horribly unhappy in Columbus. As an only child, Dena felt obliged to spend them with her parents and Christos supported the decision. These family get-togethers would include Nick's brother, Pete, his wife, Pat, and their son, Dean. But there was never anyone else included beyond those seven people. This is curious given that Greeks often include everyone they know in celebrations, both large and small. Dena remembers the constant fighting and shouting, the persistent bickering about things that didn't matter. Nick and Pete would inevitably end up arguing about something. It was unpleasant. Amelia never said a word. Neither did Dena or Christos. They just sat there and watched to avoid stepping into the crosshairs.

But there was one unusual Christmas when Nick and Amelia did invite their son-in-law's parents to join them. It was pleasant enough, but only because there was company, outsiders. Nick would make sure not to embarrass himself by creating a scene. He knew how much his daughter loved her in-laws. An argument could push her closer to them, something he would not gamble to reinforce. He seethed with jealousy on that score.

Both couples, Nick and Amelia and Costas and Maria, were from the same area of Greece. They all came from small villages near to and around the legendary city of Sparta. They were all Tsintzinians. They made idle conversation and, at some point, Maria casually asked about Dena's young life, including the circumstances of her birth.

Nick told her that an uncle, who was a doctor, Dr. Grigoris, found Dena in an orphanage. Her mother, a teenager, had died in childbirth, and was not married. Her father was non-existent and no one knew the relationship between mother and father. The orphanage had sent a photo of the infant to Nick and Amelia, and soon after the couple made the arrangements to bring her to the United States.

"Where was she born," Maria asked. "Sparta," said Nick, "an orphanage in Sparta." Maria thought about it for a moment and said, "I know Sparta well. I was born there. I don't remember any orphanage in Sparta. In fact, I am *sure* there was no orphanage there." But Nick insisted that there was. "Maybe it had been destroyed," he said, "and you don't remember it."

Maria thought for a moment about not pressing the issue. She paused, but persisted saying, "Look, I know for sure there was never any orphanage in my hometown." Nick shot back growing angrier with every passing second. "You don't know what the hell you are talking about," he said, incredulous and greatly offended. Who did she think she was, talking to Nick Polites like that, he thought. But Maria stood her ground. "I **do know** what I am talking about," she shot back, undeterred.

The conversation began to escalate and spiral out of control as Nick explained in rapid fire his securing a baby from Sparta.

"We sent money to Dena's uncle, who was a doctor."

"We asked him to find a baby."

"He found Dena and we paid to bring her to us."

"She went from an orphanage in Sparta to Athens."

"Then she was brought to New York and we brought her to Columbus."

He almost appeared exhausted defending the story.

The exchange was difficult. Uncomfortable. Suspicious. It gave both Dena and Christos pause. "Jesus, there are red flags everywhere," Christos thought to himself.

Dena recalled all the times she had traveled to Sparta with her parents. Nick had always made a point of telling her the same story. "That mountain over there, that's where your birth mother's village is, and that is where she died," he would say pointing to it. She had believed through all those years that her very roots were in Sparta. She embraced it so much so that she even had a vanity plate made for her car. SPARTA. It was something to hold on to. One of the very few things to know for sure about her young self, which she celebrated in her own small way.

From that fateful Christmas, Nick completely turned on Dena's in-laws. They rarely saw each other again afterward. He called them names. He began to demean them at every turn. Said they were not "real Greeks." He called them *prosfiyes*, refugees, a real put-down at the time. DP's they were. Displaced persons. It is what some Greeks called other Greeks, who had come from Greece. He made a particular distinction between Greeks from Greece and American-born Greeks, who Nick felt were superior. He began to call Christos names, too. As for the orphanage in Sparta, that subject was summarily dropped. Dena left it as she always felt she had to. Nick made certain that questions and challenges to his authority would not be entertained. But it was a sliver of information that stuck with Christos and with Dena. It bothered them.

"My life was never without stress when I was in their house, when I was with them," Dena recalls. She hadn't even learned she was adopted until she was seven. "When I found out I was shocked. I was confused. Where am I from? Who am I? But I would never dare pursue the answers to those questions." Over the course of her life her feelings and questions would drift to the surface for just an instant, and then would sink back down again. She would force them down and away, afraid of how her rightful questions about her own life might be received and answered. But those questions were there. Always there. Quiet. Hiding.

In Kastania, Popi remembers it was when she was a teenager, maybe 14 or 15 years old, when she learned she had a big sister. Her mother sat her down to finally tell the awful story of their first child, Popi's sibling, who was lost to them, and about the dire mistake she thought she made entrusting the infant to caretakers. The story was hard to retell, but she wanted Popi and her brother, Giorgos, to know the truth, to know that their family was not complete.

Vasilo explained, "People said to let it go, to forget," but "you cannot forget a child that came from you, that was part of you, a person that is your blood." Popi was confused at first, surprised later, and finally delighted, telling her mother that secretly she had always wanted a sister.

"I can never forget and I will never forgive myself," she told her daughter. But Mama, Popi said, grasping her hand, we have to find her. "Did you try? Where did this happen? How did this happen?" Vasilo recounted her steps, the story, her history.

"When I became pregnant, I was banished from the village," she told her daughter.

"*Yiayia* and I left for Arta, where I gave birth."

"Your father was in prison, as you know," she continued.

"After giving birth, your *Pappou* and I went with the baby to the prison so that I could marry your father and so he could see his first-born. We were refused, never allowed to see him."

"Later we took the child to a shelter in Lake Pamvotida and returned to Kastania to see how we could live there under such pressure and intimidation."

"Your *Pappou* decided we would bring the baby home; that she was ours to love and care for, no matter the consequences."

"When we returned to the shelter, not many days later, she was gone."

That is the whole story, Vasilo told her daughter, head bowed. "There is not a single trace of her, Popi, not a paper, not a name, nothing," Vasilo quietly recounted, almost in a hushed whisper. "She is lost," her mother said, an unmistakable grief poking itself to the surface once again. "But we must always remember her," Vasilo said to her daughter. "We must pray that she is safe, that she is happy, that someone, somewhere in the world loves her, if she is even alive."

"We must pray."

And so, every night, like her mother, Popi would stand before the icons and the forever- lit candle, floating in oil, gently flickering through the red vessel, and she would recite the *"Pater imon,"* the "Our Father." But praying was not enough. Praying alone would never be enough for Popi. She would try to do something about it.

She had a sister, a sister she had always wanted, and she would not be satisfied knowing that a person was out there in the world, who belonged to her, to her family. Their family was one of five people, not four. She also could not bear the pain that her parents had suffered.

A nagging refrain for Popi over the years was refusing to believe there was no documentation noting her sister's birth. When she was 20, she decided to travel to Arta, to the General Hospital where her sister was born. She found the appropriate office and asked to see the ledger, the archival record of births at the hospital.

Old and dusty, hand-written, with a band around it to secure the frayed and fractured binding, the clerk handed her the book she wanted to examine. She began going through each page, her finger guiding her eyes to each name and date as she very intently focused on the task at hand. It was on the next page where she suspected her sister's birth would be recorded, flipping it quickly, ready again to scrutinize the names as she searched for her mother's.

Vasiliki Gyftokosta.

The next page was missing. And the next and the next. So were the following ten pages. Missing. "Where are these pages," Popi pointedly asked the clerk. "I don't know," he replied, dispassionately, casually looking up at her from his work. "But they are missing. They are ripped out of this book," Popi said with frustration, her voice rising. He didn't know and there was no one else to ask, the clerk said dismissively. Any record of her sister's birth was nonexistent. It was as if she hadn't been born at all. Dejected and feeling defeated, she returned to the village. She decided not to tell her mother.

Popi eventually went to cosmetology school and decided to move to Arta, a big city, where there was a client-base far beyond the tiny village where she grew up. She became engaged to the son of the singer in her father's small band. His name was also Giorgos. They were engaged for six years, married for five, and later divorced.

Popi's brother, George, after high school, went to a trade

school to learn heating, ventilation, and air conditioning. He became an HVAC technician and later moved to Mykonos, one of the marquee Greek islands, and worked in a photo shop.

Both children were dutiful and loved their parents. They would return often to their mountain village of Kastania to check in and make sure all was well.

Stress may have been the reason that Dena and Christos could not conceive in the short time they lived with Nick and Amelia after returning from Massachusetts. They tried. They very much wanted children to start and grow a family. Finally, they moved into their own apartment and later into a home. Dena would endure a tubal pregnancy, which she would have to abort, and then another miscarriage. Finally, she was pregnant with twin boys.

Given her previous difficulties conceiving, hers was labeled a high-risk pregnancy and so she was forced to take it easy. There was a business to run, a house to keep, and cooking to do, so her in-laws came to live with their son and his wife when the boys were born on April 14, 1995. They helped with the babies and helped at the deli, and would end up staying for five years. It was a precious gift. The boys grew very close to their grandparents. They heard and learned Greek as small boys, which Dena and Christos believed was good for them.

The boys were named Costa and Nicko. It is tradition for Greeks to name sons after grandfathers and Christos and Dena complied. One named for his father, the other named for hers. But even babies, his own grandsons, were not enough to soften the attitude and behavior of Nick. He behaved badly and overtly favored one son over the other. Of course, it was Nicko, his namesake, who was his favorite.

Although the boys were twins, they were as different as fraternal twins could be. Costa was shy and not as socially comfortable. Nicko was rambunctious, outgoing and always smiling. Nick could not be bothered with Costa, who may have struggled in the shadow of his engaging twin brother. He did not help make it better for the boys, and especially for Costa. He was not encouraging and he did not engage Costa in the same way. In fact, he would ignore him, not even hold him, as he repeatedly gravitated to the more effervescent child.

Dena remembers that Nick would only bring gifts for the one child. She felt for her sweet Costa and challenged her father on his unfairness and hurtful behavior. "He doesn't know. He's too little," Nick shouted. "Oh, yes, he does," Dena shouted back, emboldened now as a married woman with Christos to back her up, defend her, protect her against the wall of Nick's insolence. "You cannot treat them differently," she would repeatedly say, always on the verge of tears, and hurting for her Costa.

By the time the children were three years old, in 1998, Dena's mother, Amelia, had died. She endured a long illness and Dena had taken care of her until she couldn't anymore. She reluctantly surrendered her to a nursing home. With age, Nick grew ever angrier at the world and toward his daughter. Not surprisingly, she chose not to invite him to live with her, the children, and Christos. She just couldn't bear the emotional weight of him. It had long ago become too toxic.

Instead, she convinced him to go into a nursing home where skilled practitioners could take better care of him as he further aged, reminding him that he had more than enough money to do so. Dena would come to see him with the boys, and would make sure he was getting the best care and was comfortable. She promised. Also, she assured him she would not forget him during the holidays either.

On one such occasion, when Dena visited Nick with the children, he was particularly agitated. Dena had to get home to her husband who was tending to the business alone. She wanted the boys to see their father, to have dinner with him before they went to bed. Nick made a scene. He shouted at her through the car window on the passenger side, "Why don't you bring the boys over more often?" The boys were in the back seat. Their backs stiffened. They sat erect in their car seats as they reacted to the rising animosity in his voice. They were silent.

"You always take them to your in-laws. Why not here more? Why? **WHY**?" Nick's head and shoulders protruded into the car. Dena was all too familiar with this ugliness, this aggression. "I snapped then and there," she said. "Go ahead and hit me. **HIT ME**. I swear to God you will never see them again." She was shaking and crying and trying to sooth her frightened sons all at once as she pulled away. This was the father she knew all too well. This was the father she had learned to despise, resent, and now even to hate.

Dena on her way to America, 1959.

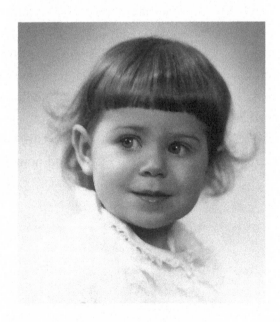

The first photo of Dena
in the United States, 1959.

First photo of Christos Poulias and Dena Polites,
August 1980 at the Washington, D.C. National Zoo.

Mr. and Mrs. Christos Poulias
July 12, 1981, Columbus, Ohio.

Dena Poulias and her adoptive parents,
Amelia and Nick Polites, circa 1985.

Dena and her mother, Vasilo.

The boys, Costa and Nicko, with Yiayia
and Pappou, Vasilo and Zachari.

Dena and her parents, Vasiliki
and Apostolos Papazacharis, April 2000.

Dena and her grandmother, Constantina, 2001.

Zachari, playing his clarino,
with grandsons, Costa and Nicko.

From left: Popi, Giorgos, Dena, Zachari,
Vasilo and Christos.

Dena and her father, Zachari.

Dena and her father, Zachari.

Costa, Dena, Nicko, Christos and Meli
at Mykonos Kuzina in Naples, Florida.

Christos, Nicko, Dena and Costa
at home in Florida.

Nick's life did not end well and he left no parting affection or regard for his daughter or her husband. In fact, he left one, final, hurtful insult in the wake of his death. For years he had operated a very successful blueprint business, and with it he had purchased that shopping center where Niki's Restaurant and Deli was located. He collected rent from the other stores. His accountant suggested that he not sell it. "Instead," he said, "why not sell it to your daughter and her husband for a nominal price? It will be a continual source of income for them over the years and it will serve as a no-tax gift for you," the accountant explained. Nick told him he thought it was a good idea and he told Dena and Christos of this plan about which they were very grateful, happy, and relieved. Their life was certainly to be made easier because of his generosity.

But, another betrayal.

They later learned that Nick had sold the shopping center right out from under them, even as they were on their way to sign the papers. He told them he had gotten a cash offer "from a Jew," he said. "Eight-hundred-thousand dollars. That's a lot of money, so I took it," he said dispassionately, without a shred of guilt or remorse. No apology. No explanation. He hurt them again. But there was one thing more to come.

On his actual death bed Nick decided to change his will. He gave the lion's share of his money to the church, to his brother, and to his nephew. He did leave some money for both of his grandsons. But Dena got nothing. She was written out of the will in an 11th- hour betrayal.

Not. My. Blood.

It was in a hospital room where Nick spent his final days. His heart problems and asthma had grown worse, and so had his temperament. He had been moved from the nursing home because he required intensive care. It was at the hospital when the family's priest, Father John Stavropoulos, came to say a prayer and give him what was certain to be a final communion. But there was not to be a divine reckoning, a coming to Jesus, to ask for forgiveness, to ask God to save his soul, and to atone for his sins, his cruelty over many years toward his wife, his daughter, her husband, and his grandsons. There was no fear and no warmth and no tears for the years of abuse. There was no grand revelation for Nick. None of any kind.

Nick had chosen another path, a different path. He yelled and screamed at the priest and berated him, which could be heard down the hall and through the plate glass window in his room. He didn't want communion. He didn't want prayers. He wanted out of the goddamned hospital.

The priest refused to take the abuse and left the room, shaking his head as he slowly walked down the sterile tile hallway, his footsteps echoing loudly. He delicately carried the holy chalice covered with a red velvet cloth trimmed in gold braids that he had brought for the sacrament, only to encounter Dena and Christos who had come to visit.

Father John told them, "I could not give him communion. I'm sorry. While he is in that frame of mind, with that attitude, he just cannot and should not receive." Dena and Christos understood perfectly. He told the couple, "I may come back to try again, but I can't promise you that I will. I am sorry."

Dena and Christos said their goodbyes to Father John and reluctantly went to see Nick. They, too, were met with anger. He was angry he was in the hospital. Angry at Dena for not taking care of him in her home. Angry that he was not in control, and that those around him refused to do what he demanded of them. The couple did not, could not stay long. They had taken about all they could, having done more than they should have over the years. They were exhausted and so very tired of enduring the constant barrage of insults and rage.

A week later, March 4, 1999, just 66 days after Dena lost her mother, Nick died alone in the middle of the night. The phone rang in the dead of night to pierce the silence of that hour, which brings respite and rest for some, agony and worry to others.

For Dena and Christos, it was the much-needed rest that was disturbed. Rattled awake, they were called to the hospital at two in the morning. Dena remembered those things that you recall in the moment when death has come. "His mouth was open. I remember that. One hand rested on his chest. His arm was alongside his body with the I-V still in it. I didn't go near him. I didn't cry."

His funeral was relatively large. People knew Nick Polites. He had been a larger-than-life figure in the community. After all, he had been a businessman of some wealth and influence, and was a big donor to the church and to other Greek interests, including the AHEPA. Dena remembers that while people expressed their sympathies at the funeral, they also quietly acknowledged they knew Nick was a difficult man. One said, "Too bad he didn't die before your mother." Another simply said, "Finally, you are free." "I did feel free," Dena admitted. "He was dead and there was relief in that for me."

Perhaps there was an acceptance and a realization, too, as she contemplated his life, now over, that he was the person who had been her tormentor. He was not the loving father that she longed for and needed. Not her protector. Not anyone who made her feel safe. With his death came a physical separation beyond the emotional. This was a disunion. It was the severing of a tenuous connection that was never really there anyway, because she was continually reminded of her difference over the course of her entire life. She was often treated like an outsider. Dena felt little, except for one thing. And it was something that she finally accepted, for herself, over the course of all those years.

Not. My. Blood.

Dena was thoughtful as the days passed after Nick died. She thought about her own life and her place in the world, beyond her immediate family. She remembered the argument about the orphanage in Sparta. She thought about how angry Nick became when his story had been challenged. It pulled at her.

She also recalled an article she had read in *People Magazine* about Greek adoption practices in the 1950s, entitled "*A Sense of Belonging.*" She made no meaningful connection then. It hadn't resonated until now. She rummaged through the stack of newspapers and magazines to find what she was looking for. She slowly read through the article over a cup of coffee and thought about her own life.

Birthright.

Who am I?

To whom do I belong?

Losing the set of parents who raised you, no matter if the experience was positive or negative, often gives breath and space to thoughts about the parents who bore you. For adoptees there can be an unmistakable void. Questions left unanswered. What were the circumstances of their birth, their life at first breath? The narratives of adoptees are often tangled, severed, and managed with very little thought to the life of the child, who is being denied their biological history, the circumstances of how they came into the world, and what led to their being given away, orphaned, abandoned. Infants, babies, children— they are human beings, little people, who will someday have pasts of their own— pasts they will want knowledge of and details about.

They deserve the stories of their own lives— truthful, accurate, and conveyed with care and sensitivity, maybe even imparted with love.

Dena's entire life had been appropriated by a dominant father, who never embraced her as his. He had actively denied her establishing and understanding her own, true identity. Her own voice had been silenced, suppressed out of fear, out of intimidation. Dena has had regrets about not confronting him over the years. "I had no guts," she said, but "I was so afraid of him. I didn't want to get hit." And Amelia, she said, "just got used to it and would say 'that's just the way he is,' Dena."

Years later, looking back, Dena's story seemed more insidious now. She was coming to terms with her life and Christos pressed for more, advocating for the life and identity of his wife; for the truth. He became her voice. He became her champion, her advocate. "I love her," he said. "I was always going to defend and protect my wife."

"But about Nick I grew tired and angry over the years," Christos said. "I was sick of seeing Dena treated the way she was. She was lied to. I was lied to. **WE** were lied to." For Christos, Nick's death triggered a host of feelings and memories. There were two incidents, specifically.

The first was their return from their honeymoon in the Bahamas. The couple had brought back a Hawaiian shirt for Nick. A gift from their trip. Nick threw it to the ground screaming, "That's it? After all I did for you, including the wedding I paid for? Shame on you both!" His face reddened with misplaced anger. Christos thought, "There is something wrong with this picture. We had just come back from **our** honeymoon. We had thought of him and brought back a fun gift. It was appropriate, but it was never enough. Never."

And there was another time that Christos will never forget. "I don't remember the argument exactly, I don't recall what he was upset about, but something had triggered him. I remember that out in the street, as we were leaving the house, Nick followed us to the car. He pushed Dena to the ground and he hit her. I remember he said, 'You are nothing and not my daughter.'" We left, of course, Christos said. "Couldn't get out of there fast enough, but I told him he better never lay a hand on her again."

"To be honest," Christos said with an audible sigh, "I don't remember much, if any, good about him. He was not a nice man, and whenever we were around him, we were terrified of arguments that would inevitably break out. There was never a happy holiday with him and rarely a happy time in their home. It's very sad and I take no pleasure in saying any of these things."

It was time for Dena and Christos to confront and sort out her father's affairs. There were issues with the estate and Nick's brother, Pete, was going to challenge the will even though Dena was the sole legal heir to any inheritance beyond the will. He had already gotten money from his brother's estate, mandated by the will, but now wanted even more. He wanted Dena's house, the house she grew up in. Not my blood, not **our** blood, he thought about Dena. Because she was not *of* them, he thought, she was entitled to nothing.

Dena would need her adoption papers for the legal fight ahead. She would defend her right to the family home. She had a birth certificate, her naturalization certificate, and her United States passport. Dena and Christos did not understand the contradiction they had in their hands at the time.

It was Christos, who ventured downtown to the Franklin Municipal Courthouse in Columbus, Ohio, and turned over the paperwork to the clerk in order to secure the record of Dena's adoption. The clerk looked at the birth certificate with some consternation. She looked up at Christos after examining the document saying, "This is an unusual birth certificate." "It doesn't look right," she told him. "It doesn't look clean. It doesn't even look *valid*," she said.

The birth certificate, entitled Certificate of Live Birth, resembled a blueprint copy of a document. Dena was familiar with paper that looked like this. It resembled what her father produced in his very successful blueprint business. This document noted that Dena had been born to Amelia and Nicholas Polites on May 5, 1958 in the town of Sparta, Greece. It noted that the "usual residence of the mother" was Columbus, Ohio. No time of birth. No weight or height. The father was listed as Nick Polites. The birth certificate was obviously manufactured. Also, if Dena was born to a US citizen or citizens, why had they filed a petition for her naturalization?

The clerk retreated to the archival files in the courthouse, but returned to say that there were no papers, no adoption records of any kind in their possession related to a Dena Polites. They were sorry.

Desperate times. Desperate measures.

Christos decided to try the Federal Bureau of Investigation, the FBI. He presented Dena's passport, her naturalization paper, and her birth certificate, the same papers, all that he had, and explained the story of Dena coming to America. The FBI checked their files, the archives, whatever it had, but came up empty. "I'm sorry," the clerk said. "I cannot find anything on her. No trace of her. According to our records, she does not exist." Christos chuckled to himself as he walked away and thought, "She doesn't exist? Of course, she exists. She's my wife, the mother of my two sons."

Christos next took the same paperwork to the Ohio Department of Health in Columbus. Nothing. Christos returned to the courthouse and the same clerk to ask what other options were available. "You've exhausted them," she told him. "We have nothing and there is nothing more we can do. There is nowhere else to go." "Please take my phone number," Christos said, as he jotted it down for her. "If you find anything, think of anything more we can do, please call," and he left it at that.

A day or two later, Chris and Dena were at home relaxing with glasses of wine after they left work. It was quiet, the way late in the day can be. The phone rang, disturbing the silence between them. Christos picked it up. The voice at the other end said, "Are you Chris, the husband of Dena Polites?" "I am", he replied. "Who is this?" "This is the records department of the courthouse downtown," the voice said. "We have some information for you. Can you come to the courthouse?"

The first thing the next morning, the couple went downtown together. They were met by the same woman who had helped Christos previously. She greeted them. "Wait one minute, please," she said. She went to a desk at the back of the office and returned immediately with a large, sealed manila envelope. She handed it to them saying, "I'm sorry. We just found this. There is nothing more other than this, and we don't even know if what's inside will help you."

They thanked her and nervously looked at the envelope wondering if it did hold some secret, some clue, some code to unravel the puzzle of Dena's life. But they would not get their hopes up as the elevator gently took them to the ground-floor of the building. They stood next to each other in silence, looking at the ceiling, at the floor, and at the illuminated numbers as they descended floor to floor, as people do in elevators. The envelope. Dena held it with care as they silently drove home, rushing into the house, now anxiously ripping the seal.

What's in a name? In this case, everything.

Vasiliki Gyftokosta.

There it was. Finally. A record noting Dena's birth, which included the name of a birth mother. "Oh, my God," said Christos. "It's your mother's name. Right here." They both stared at the document, and at the name with trepidation, with elation.

Dena was born in the city of Arta, not Sparta. The envelope did not contain a Greek birth certificate. Instead, it contained an Application for Immigrant Visa, which included Dena's birthdate, birthplace, birth mother's name, and her village. It noted a foster home provided by PIKPA, the Greek national welfare institution that kept its main offices at 5 Ippokratous Street in Athens. Dena was brought to the United States on an El Al flight by a non-descript woman named only as *"Fotini."* There was a note on a document from the U.S. Department of Justice stating, "We have no papers proving adoption."

Another document was from the Ohio Department of Health, attached to the Petition for Adoption, which noted Dena's name before her adoption, Baby Girl Gyftokosta, and her name after as Dena Maria Polites. There were no documents, in any form, noting that the birth mother voluntarily relinquished her child.

But there **was something** disturbing, and even a little sinister, which was insinuated in one of the documents. Christos said, "There was clearly an indication that someone wanted these papers lost or destroyed, and it seemed like a directive that came from someone higher up. It was not explicit, but when we read it, it raised more suspicion. Nothing was right about any of these papers." They also had known that Amelia, the adoptive mother of Dena, had at one time worked for Governor James A. Rhodes of Ohio.

Dena's infant life was nefariously ensnared in a systemic movement which drained Greece of its infants, babies, and children to adoption outside the country. This movement was instigated by war, poverty, and dependence upon other powerful forces, both external and internal. The wealthy and powerful, the well-heeled and influential, always seemed to know best and exerted pressure on vulnerable, wounded Greece to do the things **they** may have wanted it to do. This pressure came at the expense and mercy of the helpless and defenseless, who in the 1940's, were starving and homeless in the battered country. According to a February 9, 1942 TIME Magazine article, Greece was described as "the hungriest country in the world."

It was post wars, two of them in succession, between 1940 and 1949. Both had ravaged Greece, a small, poor country, which suffered greatly through the late 40s and 50s, not really gaining its footing until the mid-60s. One war was put upon it; the other came from political division within.

Like the other countries of Europe, Greece was hit hard by the onslaught and cruelty of Nazism and Fascism that devastated the continent during World War II. It absorbed much of the violence, which was enacted by the Germans and, later during the Civil War, that of Greek pitted against Greek. It was an ugly chapter in the country's history.

The Axis powers, Italy, Germany and Bulgaria were the forces initially behind the destruction of Greece. The Italians first invaded Greece in October 1940, but the Hellenic army managed to push the aggressors back into Albania.

While Greece was preoccupied with the Italians defending the northern borders, Germany circumvented the conflict, and in April 1941 headed south to invade the mainland, then Crete, the southernmost and largest of the Greek islands.

By June 1941, Greece had fallen and was invaded, defeated, and now occupied by Germany. A seminal event was the German army hoisting the swastika flag adopted by Adolf Hitler and the Nazi party, on the flat, thick stones of the Acropolis, just steps from the iconic Parthenon. The grotesque ceremony, a horrifying sight, replete with German soldiers in attendance, was anathema to freedom-loving Greeks and other democracies throughout the world.

The war brought utter devastation. Villages and cities were bombed and ruined. Famine swept the land. It also robbed Greece of some 80,000 Greek-Jews by genocide in some 31 different communities sprinkled throughout the country, ostensibly wiping out Greek-Jewry, a precious population, which brought diversity to the predominantly Orthodox Christian country.

By best estimates, before Greece's civil war (1946-1949) and because of World War II, "the total number of Greek war orphans (who had lost one or both parents) was estimated to be 340,000 to 375,000."

World War II engendered the subsequent Civil War.

With the Greek government in exile during the German occupation of Greece, a power vacuum formed with political rivalries taking shape, right against left. The army of the Greek government was backed by the United Kingdom and then by the United States. And the Democratic Army of Greece, the DSE, the military arm of the Communist Party, the KKE, was (nominally) supported by the Soviet Bloc.

Exacerbating the already toxic political climate, was that the British helped to "reinstall the Greek royal house against the will of large segments of the Greek population." While the Greeks resisted the Nazi invasion, the royals had fled to Egypt and South Africa for safekeeping. During the Civil War, however, the monarchy returned, and Queen Frederica had begun establishing camps and shelters for the orphans of Greece. They were called *paidopoleis*, child cities, and were state-sponsored. She meant well, but it didn't necessarily go well. Further, many Greeks were not happy about the return of the royals. The Queen had promoted and also helped manage the lives of orphans in country and their flow out of the country.

"By 1950, one out of eight children was orphaned," according to the Greek Ministry of Social Welfare. Greece had become "a nation of orphans," and between 1948 and 1962, "had the highest annual per capita adoption ratio in the world." Further, the country was being infantilized by powerbrokers, with the United States in the lead, which helped Greece rebuild and had poured money into the country to that end. Help from the United States came at a high price, though.

Ostensibly, it knew better what was best for "helpless" Greece and it also knew what was best for its destitute orphaned children. "Adopted children," the U.S. thought, would grow up in a democratic and peaceful new country that prized traditional family life." America came to the rescue, the hero of the Greek story, which in reality was an utter tragedy— the export of its children, the future of Greece.

Americans, preferably Greek-Americans, would be better-suited to care for the orphaned children of Greece, giving them lives they never could have dreamed of. Plus, Greeks could give Greek-born children "the continuity of their heritage in language, culture and religion." Without considering mother or child, or Greece itself, thousands of its infants, babies and children, were exported. Activist, labor specialist, and member of the Greek parliament, Maria Svolou, was critical of the "export of Greek children" as "unacceptable." She said the "flow of Greek children to America" was left "unchecked."

Some adoptions of that time were simple, legal adoptions, and private. Others were expensive and complicated. Many were illegal and others had criminal overtones. A profit motive had been created to move babies and children from one place to another in country and also far beyond Greek borders, internationally. But the issue was more importantly that of human rights. "Birth mothers and adoptive families were routinely deceived in this transnational scene of baby brokering, which left children without protection."

Two organizations stand out in the brokering and "care" of Greek babies outside the country. The first in Greece is PIKPA, the Patriotic Institution for Social Welfare and Awareness. It began in 1914 as a "women's philanthropic organization assisting and caring for poor families." In 1951, however, it began caring for "unprotected children," under the auspices of the Queen.

The organization handled domestic adoptions, but in the 1950s began arranging international adoptions as well. Rather than strengthen child welfare services at home, also giving support to birth mothers, international adoption became "not merely an alternative," but was "a ready-made solution" to the burgeoning problem of orphaned children and mothers, who allegedly could not care for them.

Part of PIKPA's mandate was to place Greek children in Greek homes, ensuring that those children would be raised in the Greek Orthodox faith and would be immersed in the culture of their birth as they grew up. PIKPA also provided foster homes where children would be cared for until their adoptions were finalized, and the children flown or shipped off.

In the United States it was the AHEPA, the American Hellenic Educational Progressive Association. The organization was created in Atlanta, Georgia in 1922 "to combat bigotry, hatred and discrimination" at the hands of the Ku Klux Klan, which also terrorized Greeks and Greek-owned businesses. It later became an organization that celebrated Hellenic ideals while also promoting philanthropy. It was and is well-endowed. It was and is powerful and it has grown to some 400 chapters across the United States, Canada, and Europe.

Part of its philanthropy was helping to place Greek-born babies in Greek-American homes. It searched for babies in

Greece to place in temporary foster homes or in permanent ones. In fact, the organization was accredited by the U.S. State Department as a "volunteer refugee service agency," called the AHEPA Refugee Relief Committee. The organization even advertised in the Greek-American press. But the AHEPA's adoption processes were shady, loose, and inexact in terms of why and how biological mothers were relinquishing their children, in screening orphanages, foster homes, and permanent adoptive homes. Applying to adopt a child was relatively easy. Requirements to submit certain "documentary certifications" were being waived and AHEPA leaders were pressuring Washington to "cut even more red tape" and to issue "blanket assurances" on "behalf of its refugee sponsors and adopters."

The AHEPA's involvement in U.S.-bound adoptions may have begun as a charitable act, fulfilling the dreams of childless couples, maybe with every good intention. But the demand for babies in the United States "outstripped supply" and the AHEPA capitalized on the situation. It became an operation, a lucrative broker of babies, and controlled a "near monopoly" on the flow of children from Greece.

According to the 1962 Report of the Committee on Matrimonial and Family Laws in the State of New York, "commercialized traffic in children was taking place" between Greece and the United States. The Report further stated that "the baby selling racketeers have practically secured a monopoly" and have "moved the recognized social agencies out of the picture." Money motivated those who could move babies from one place to another, grease the palms of lawyers and mid-level administrators, orphanage directors, and maybe even priests. Documents were "concocted" in some cases and in others "forged."

Some babies were stolen from their birth mothers. Some babies were "re-registered as foundlings and some parents were told their baby had died, but were not shown a body or a death certificate." Further, "numerous mothers of children born out of wedlock were being denied any meaningful consent in the adoption proceedings."

In the case of Dena Poulias, there is no hard evidence that her adoption was manipulated by or arranged for by the AHEPA, but her journey from birth to the United States is highly suspect. Circumstantial.

Her adoptive father, Nick Polites, was an active member of the AHEPA, who gave generous donations to the organization over many years. He routinely attended its annual conventions.

A record of Dena's birth at the hospital in Arta was destroyed. Why? By whom?

An original Greek birth certificate cannot be found for Baby Girl Gyftokosta.

The shelter at Lake Pamvotida, where Dena was taken for temporary care, was likely paid to classify baby Dena as abandoned or orphaned. She was relinquished to an intermediary without explanation, without record, and without permission from either surviving parent.

Dena's journey from Lake Pamvotida to Athens is completely unknown. Who took her to Athens?

"*Fotini*" brought her to the United States. Who was *Fotini* and for whom did she work?

Or, was she just an ordinary passenger on the same flight as baby Dena, who had been asked or who had just offered to keep an eye on the baby?

The "birth certificate" that Dena's adoptive parents had in their possession was a fake. The documentation providing the name of her birth mother is only found on documents issued in Greece.

Those documents revealed scant information about Dena's identity, but were deliberately hidden from her.

The Governor of Ohio knew the AHEPA. The husband of his secretary, Amelia Polites, Dena's adoptive mother, was an active member. The Governor had elevated a Supreme Counsellor of the AHEPA from Cleveland Chapter 36, Greek-American Judge John M. Manos, to the Ohio Court of Appeals.

And in any reading of the history of AHEPA, on its own website and in archival documents readily available, it is clear that the organization celebrated its strong and deep ties to politics and politicians in both state and federal government.

AHEPA's past would haunt the future.

Dena's past began to emerge after the revelation of one single name, the name of her birth mother, Vasiliki Gyftokosta. It had been lost and buried for nearly 40 years. It was the key to the story and circumstances of her birth.

Dena was frozen, maybe even frightened, her feelings never allowed to surface because of years of ingrained fear, having been silenced into submission for so long. Christos would drive the search for Dena's mother. Was she even alive? And if so, where was she?

It was back to the *People Magazine* article where there was a thread to a lead, which the couple would pursue. They read, "Hundreds, perhaps thousands of poverty-stricken couples and unwed mothers left their infants in children's shelters or hospitals for safekeeping. Later, when they tried to reclaim their babies, many were told the children were gone or had died. Many of the children had been sold, shipped to America and other countries, where unwitting couples paid steep black-market fees." A Greek television program broke the story after "a Greek lawyer raised questions about her own adoption records."

The program led Christos and Dena to one Litsa Kyrellis, who peripherally worked with the program and was living in Miami. She had become salvation to many people, who were searching for their biological relatives, a modern-day sleuth for Greek adoptees. They found her number, placed a call, and explained their story. Kyrellis agreed to take their case. They gave her the name of Dena's biological mother and fed her what little information they had. Of course, they would pay for any expense incurred during the search, which from this point on, did not take long.

Even though Vasiliki's home village was listed as Kastania, Kyrellis began in the city of Arta, where, chances were, she thought, young women, who had given birth out of wedlock, would likely have migrated to start new lives, far from stigma and judgment. There were 15 Gyftokostases' listed in the white pages. She dialed each one of them and had one simple question, "Do you know Vasiliki Gyftokosta?" For several there was no answer. Some didn't know. But there was one woman.

"Hello, I am trying to reach a Vasiliki Gyftokosta," Kyrellis dryly recited.

"This is Vasiliki Gyftokosta," the voice at the other end said. Kyrellis, now fully alert, lifted her chin from the hand that had been holding it, and took the phone into her other hand, which had been cradled between her ear and shoulder.

"Vasiliki Gyftokosta?" she repeated. "Yes."

Kyrellis told her why she was calling. This Vasiliki Gyftokosta was careful and guarded, resistant to divulge anything, not even that she was actually a cousin of the woman Kyrellis was looking for. Kyrellis realized this wasn't the right person, but felt that she knew something.

"Please," Kyrellis implored, "I need your help. It's important. This is about the life of a lost child." After some cajoling and back and forth, the woman finally relented and gave the name of a village north of Arta, the tiny village called Kastania.

"Try there," she said. "Here is someone you can call." She shared a name and telephone number.

Kyrellis reached and spoke to a Vangelis Katsanos in the village. To him, she recounted the story, all that she knew. "Yes," he told her, "I know the story quite well."

"But you are now searching for Vasiliki Papazachari," Vangelis told Kyrellis. "She is here. She lives here and she married," he said. "She married the father of the child who was lost."

Kyrellis paused, lifting her head a little higher. Had she heard it all correctly? She carefully repeated back to him what she had just heard. "The parents of this child, married? The biological father of this baby married the mother who gave birth to her? And they are both alive?" Kyrellis asked, now wide-eyed.

"Yes," he said. "They married in 1973. They are here and very much alive." He willingly gave Kyrellis the phone number of Vasiliki and Apostolos Papazacharis. She could hardly believe what she had heard.

Vangelis Kastanos, the man she had just spoken to, was Dena's uncle, the husband of her mother's sister, Stamatia.

Kyrellis told him, "Well, that lost child is no longer lost, and is looking for her mother." With that, Vangelis slammed down the phone and ran to his sister-in-law's home, unable to contain what would be the biggest story the village had heard since the disappearance of the baby more than 40 years ago.

"*Nai. Embros.*" Yes, hello.

"Hello. My name is Litsa Kyrellis. I am calling from the United States."

There was silence at the other end of the phone.

"Are you Vasiliki Gyftokosta, now Vasiliki Papazachari," asked Kyrellis.

"Yes," Vasiliki said softly and with nervous anticipation.

"Did you have a child in the 1950's? A baby girl, born on May 5, 1958, whom you had lost, who disappeared," Kyrellis continued with quiet deliberation and care.

"Yes," Vasiliki said as she covered her mouth and closed her eyes tightly.

"I am calling on behalf of a woman in the United States, who is looking for her mother, Vasiliki Gyftokosta, now Vasiliki Papazachari. Is that you," Kyrellis concluded.

"My God," Vasiliki said in Greek, as she lost control and her composure. She began to weep. Overcome, she hung up the phone and fainted as she fell to the floor.

Kyrellis immediately called back and this time it was Zacharis, who instantly picked up the phone as he was simultaneously trying to revive his wife. She repeated the story to Zacharis as he asked in rapid-fire, questions about the woman to whom Kyrellis was referring.

"How is she? Where is she? Who took her?" He also expressed shock and disbelief. "Are you sure about this?" he stammered.

And in a sweet, poignant moment, he quietly asked, "What is her name?"

"Dena," Kyrellis responded. "Her name is Constantina. Dena."

Zacharis looked up as if to thank God, and thought of his mother-in-law, Vasilo's mother, Constantina.

Dena.

Kyrellis explained that his daughter did not know yet that she had located her parents, and would need to carefully reveal the news to her. Kyrellis asked the couple questions about their own life and family. They both answered through tears, sharing the receiver of the phone between them. She also gave the couple the telephone number of Dena and Christos, but asked them to wait for a few days before calling so that Kyrellis could explain things to them first. She knew that Dena, too, would be in shock. They agreed, but kept repeating, and repeating again, that they knew someday their daughter would return to them.

It was Christos who answered when Kyrellis called. "Tell Dena to sit down," she told him. "Maybe you should tell her the news as I tell it to you, Chris."

Christos listened and kept repeating the words, "Oh, my God, oh, my God."

"Dena," he said, "sit down." She did.

"Your mother is alive and well. She still lives in Kastania, near Arta, where you were born," he said. With that first bit of news, Dena could hardly breathe.

"WHAT," Christos asked in a louder voice, gripping the phone a little tighter. "Are you sure? OK."

"Dena," he continued, "Your mother and father are married! To each other. They have been married since 1973. They have never forgotten you, but there was no trace of your disappearance, which is why they couldn't find you."

Dena sat silently and kept nodding slowly, acknowledging that she was hearing and understanding. Carefully, she stood from where she was seated and took steps to where she always went when there was something important to think about, staring out the big picture window to the backyard at nothing in particular.

The child who had been raised as an only child has a brother and a sister. They are full biological siblings, Christos told her. Her brother, Giorgos, was born in 1974. Her sister, Popi, was born in 1976. "You are their big sister," he said as his eyes welled with tears.

Dena grew up with one aunt and one uncle on either side of her adoptive family. She has three adoptive first cousins. Christos described the next bit of news as a bombshell. Dena's mother is one of seven siblings, four girls and three boys. Her father is the youngest of five, all sisters. Dena has 27 biological cousins. First cousins!

This was all difficult to process. Christos took his wife in his arms, holding her tightly. Never in a million years did she think any day like today would have occurred. Litsa Kyrellis explained that she had given her parents their telephone number and said to expect a call from them in the next few days.

Dena would need those days to collect herself, she thought. What would she say? What would she do? Her mother, her father were strangers, but she was part of each of them. She was nervous, happy, and sad all at the same time, a cascade of emotions that needed sorting, that needed making sense of.

Vasilo and Zacharis could not wait a week or even another day. They had waited long enough, over forty years, for their daughter. The next day at mid-afternoon, Columbus, Ohio time, which was late at night in Greece, Vasilo placed the call. Christos picked up the phone.

"Are you Christos Poulias," she asked in Greek.

"I am," he answered.

"I am the mother of your wife," she said, shaking and struggling to speak through her tears. Dena backed up as she listened to her husband's side of the conversation, a churn of feelings, including fear and joy and sick to her stomach. There was a barrage of questions, first from Vasilo.

"How is she? Where do you live?"

Next, Zacharis got on the phone as his wife stepped away trying to gain control of her heart, which was pounding, racing. Calm, quiet and steady as was his nature, he asked Christos if he knew what had happened to her.

"Did she have a good life? Did they treat her well? We knew we would find her again someday," he said. "We know she is our daughter," he said with certainty.

"Dena," he said her name out loud for the first time. "She is our daughter." There was silence, and then the sound of crying. All were shocked. And joyful. And in disbelief.

Christos waved Dena closer to him as she slowly edged her way to the phone. Such an odd feeling speaking to the people whom you came from, unable to say much, not knowing what to say, but uttering something benign, neither personal nor remote. She remembered a simple "Hello, how are you? I don't believe it." They were careful with her, too, also not quite knowing what to say, but they casually chatted, elation just below the surface, but measured. Controlled. Christos would later describe that first conversation as affectionate. Dena was in a daze and has little memory of it.

Christos did not want to offend these newly found in-laws, but he still asked, very delicately, whether they would be open to taking a DNA test, the two of them, just to make certain. Dena, he promised, would do the same. Immediately they agreed, fully understanding the request. They would go to the nearest place to give samples and send them. They asked for photographs. Dena asked for the same.

It was November 1999.

The photographs plodded their way through the international post while dozens of relatives were calling Columbus, Ohio from Kastania and from Athens. The DNA tests had been taken on both sides. One was being evaluated at a DNA lab in Columbus. The other two, at a DNA lab in Athens. Dena would describe the process as weeks of torture. What if it wasn't a match? What if there was some kind of crazy mistake? A last minute, profound disappointment?

Meanwhile, photos and letters arrived sporadically over the next several weeks. Dena would study each one, carefully tracing each face to see who, if anyone, looked like her. There were not many visible similarities, which worried her a little. But from photos how much can you really tell, she thought. What a thrill to see the people from whom she came, though. Her brother. Her sister. Her aunts and uncles, cousins, and a little woman she could not quite make out. She saw glimpses of the village, the place that was truly her ancestral village, and finally knowing for certain that she was born in Arta, not Sparta. She had the vanity plate on her car changed. Sparta without the S-P. It was a small thing, but it meant something to Dena.

Dena and Christos also sent photos of Dena as a baby, as a little girl, a teenager, a young woman, a bride, a mother. All the years they had missed, absent, were memorialized in photographs, moments, pieces of a life, frozen in time. And they sent photos of their sons, the only grandchildren of Vasilo and Zacharis. They wept as they studied them. Vasilo touched the faces, her fingers gently gliding over them, later sharing them with the villagers, anyone who came to talk about their lost daughter, now found, and her grandchildren. She was *Yiayia*, grandmother, and Zacharis was now *Pappou*, grandfather. *Yiayia* and *Pappou*. They are terms of endearment as much as they identify relations. For decades their pain had been great, unbearable, but now it had vanished and they would focus not on what was lost, but what had been restored.

February 14, 2000—Valentine's Day.

It was the day the DNA tests arrived. Nervous, holding her breath, Dena cautiously opened the envelope. It was a match and she finally, completely exhaled for the first time, it seemed, since November. She called the village and told her parents they would be planning their first trip to Kastania. They decided to be there for Easter.

The thought of it gave Dena both joy and trepidation. Her life would finally have closure and peace. But what would they think of her? Would they like her? Would they like each other? What would they talk about? She stopped her mind from racing and smiled thinking, after 40 years of living, on both sides, there was plenty to talk about!

In Kastania, Dena's parents were planning for a homecoming and a celebration! A child was coming back to where she belonged, to people who had longed for her and had felt the deepest agony after losing her, and for lacking any information about her, including whether she even survived.

Zacharis was busy planning an extension on their modest mountain village home. His daughter and son-in-law were coming and so were his grandsons. They would need more room, and he wanted them to be comfortable. As much as he could, he wanted this to feel like home, to be home because it *was* her home. This was his obsession as Dena began to find her way to Kastania.

Greek Easter in the year 2000 was on April 30th. The Poulias family would be there before the holiday. The boys had just celebrated their 5th birthdays.

Dena remembers the plane ride to Athens. "I was pensive," she explained. "I didn't talk much, even though my in-laws and the boys were with us. I was lost in thought, a million miles away, and stayed pretty quiet. You know, so many thoughts go through your mind." In the glare of daylight, which seemed brighter over the towering clouds, she gazed out the window as the light gave way to dusk over the Atlantic, then gradually to the impenetrable darkness at 34,000 feet. The persistent deep humming of the jet engines churned, as the plane flew through the night, hugging the curvature of the earth toward Greece.

A California therapist in adoption therapy wrote that an adoptee's search for their roots is a way of "restoring a healthy sense of control and power back" into their lives. Stories have been taken, she wrote, adoptees being "the original victims of identity theft." Adoptees experience "the triple jeopardy of loss: of their first families, of their identities and of their ability to trust others freely and without question." There was truth in this for Dena.

She had been deliberately betrayed, and for more than four decades, but she decided to focus her energy on what she had now found, not on her sense of profound loss. She needed to prepare her mind for a reunion, and she had absolutely no idea what it was going to look like or what it was going to feel like. What she *did* know was that she did not like to be the center of attention, even though her artistry on the dance floor would always draw every eye to her. Dancing, lost in her own world, she never seemed to notice. But now, she was self-conscious about the attention she would undoubtedly get from her parents and family.

Before landing, Dena went to the bathroom to make sure she looked halfway decent after a tense flight across seven time zones. The plane was packed full of passengers. They were waking from their stupor, and as they always do before nearing touchdown, began to shift and shuffle, gathering belongings, clearing the cramped area where they were sitting, rising to take things out of the overhead bins above their seats. Christos made sure the boys were in order and checked on his parents. His stomach, too, was churning, but he didn't mention it. This was a big day. It was a day that belonged to his wife, and it had been a long time coming.

The plane landed at Ellinikon International Airport. Inside the terminal, the masses had disembarked, people from other flights as well, making their way to passport control and customs. The lines moved haltingly, but steadily, to examine documents upon entry. Their luggage came in short shrift. With chalk marks, an X, hastily marking their bags, customs waved them through without any examination. Dena and the family had no issues. Actually, it went faster than expected, which made Dena a little more nervous. The efficiency gave her less time to calm her nerves as she prepared to meet her parents— her parents, completely unknown to her less than a year ago, but every bit part of her. It was a reality so difficult to grapple with, but there was no time now to sift through any more thoughts.

The group walked away from the customs terminal, through the heavy steel doors that automatically slid open. As soon as they emerged, there was a loud cry from someone in the large group gathered ahead, in front of them, as a small woman attempted to break through security. Dena didn't hear it, but the voice said, "i kori mou," my daughter. She was held back by the security guards.

Dena and Christos searched the faces in the crowd as they moved slowly forward, pushing the cart of luggage, managing the boys with two tired, but excited parents in tow. People began to shout above the din, "i Dena mas!," our Dena! "Dena, edo." Dena, over here. Dena was shaking now. Finally, her eyes focused on a large group of maybe 40 people holding flowers, waving, and with grins as wide as their faces. They were elated, joyous as they laid eyes on a child they had never seen, lost to them for practically a lifetime. Dena was in a daze as her parents rushed toward her now.

"Mama, Baba," instinctively, were her first words as she reached out for them. Her mother could not stop touching her face, repeating the words in Greek, "my girl, my girl, you have come home." They embraced and then would look into each other's eyes. They embraced again. The tears were rolling down Dena's cheeks now. Her mother was crying, too. Her father enveloped her in his arms as he held her tight, looking at her with such deep love. His eyes, she remembered, were a well of tears. Everyone was crying now as all eyes were on Dena and her family. Christos remembers that "all hell broke loose." Everyone was crying and laughing all at the same time. They all wanted to hug Dena as one by one each told her how they were related to her.

Finally, from the back of the crowd Popi pushed her way through. Overwhelmed by the sight of her sister, she felt she had to compose herself before greeting her and so waited at the back of the crowd. "I am your little sister. I am Popi," she said barely able to speak, fighting back the tears. "Popi," Dena responded as she wept. They embraced as their father hugged them both.

Zacharis turned to greet his son-in-law and his *petherika*, his in-laws, and then scooped up both grandsons in his arms at once, kissing each of them, touching their hair and faces. "It was unbelievable," Christos said. "Just incredible." "He was so moved, so happy," Christos said, "and it was made even better because the boys instantly took to him. They called him *Pappou*." "We had shown them photos," Christos said, "and they remembered what we had told them."

It took a long time to make their way out of the terminal and into taxis and cars as they wound their way through Athens to an aunt's house where food was waiting. So were more people, friends, relatives and neighbors, who wanted to see a miracle for themselves. They ate and talked and got to know one another long into the night. There was music and some dancing. The party had spilled out into the street of the tightly packed neighborhood. Everyone, it seemed, was talking at once. Questions had generated even more questions. There was laughter and so much crying out of pure elation and relief. It was a celebration of a homecoming like no other they had been a part of. The night never seemed to end, but when it did Dena and Christos stayed at the home of relatives.

Dena had no conception of where she came from. As an infant, and only briefly, had she been to Kastania. Sparta, she had known, but it is a world away, nearly 300 miles, from remote Kastania, given the geography of Greece. One is in the far north of the country, on the mainland, and Sparta is in the far south in the Peloponnese.

The trip to Kastania was a trek. The family traveled in a caravan of cars. The roads were narrow and they twisted and turned through mountain passes via sharp switchbacks. Much of it was not paved, so the dust and rocks made for a bumpy, slow-going drive. It was easy to get nauseous on the way. Dena did feel sick, but it was a combination of the difficult roads and the next part of her journey, which was to experience her ancestral village for the first time. It was the home of her parents, and of their parents before them for their entire lives.

The village entrance came after a steep incline in the road. They parked just outside the narrow entrance and began to walk toward the *plateia*, the center of the village, toward the square. Her parents were on either side of their daughter. Dena had her arm entwined through her mother's on one side. Her Dad tenderly held her hand on the other as they walked home together. They explained to Dena that there, to the immediate left, was their home, her home, and below, the coffeehouse. "That's our *kafeneion*," her father told her as he squeezed her hand a little tighter.

A crowd of villagers steadily began to walk toward them through the *plateia*, a cacophony of voices, gradually getting louder as they approached. They smiled, some waved with nervous anticipation for the return of the lost baby, a story they had known, as well as their own, and had experienced for years through the anguish of the parents.

They began to slow their pace, though, backing off just enough to let a small, old woman walk ahead of them. She was thin, with a tired, worn face that seemed to discard the years reflected on it as she got closer and began to focus on Dena's face. Dressed in a black blouse with a dotted, long, black skirt, and a black scarf covering her hair, she held out both arms, reaching for her granddaughter. She took her face in her hands, studying it, the same way she had when she saw her for the last time, as an infant, over 40 years ago.

"Constantina," she said, as she intently looked into her eyes, as if to account for the time that had been lost. "Now, I can die peacefully," the old woman said. "Now that we have you, I can die. I have been waiting." Dena was so taken by her grandmother. Finally, someone who looked like her. They had the same eyes. Immediately after, she was swept up by the other villagers, who kept staring, in disbelief, at this Easter miracle. They all seemed to walk her to the threshold of the Papazacharis home together as the family disappeared within to continue getting acquainted.

Easter.
The resurrection.

Anastasi.

It is the commemoration, the celebration of the ascension of Christ from the grave. From his tomb. It is the highest holy day in the Orthodox calendar, which marks a rebirth and start to new life. The symbolism would not be lost on anyone in Kastania that day.

There was a palpable buzz quietly reverberating throughout the tiny village that Saturday. All of Holy Week, through Holy Saturday, is somber, but it was as if the entire village was struggling to tamp down its feelings until midnight.

The family prepared for church and a service, which typically begins late Saturday night. At midnight, the lighting of a hundred candles from the small flame of a singular one, ushers in Easter.

Vasilo thought about the night those many years ago when that mystical, brilliant light appeared to her and came toward her from across the hills. While she then stood before it, frightened, at first, she believed even more, and with all her heart now, that it was a message. She felt then that everything would be alright, that some good would come to her family. But what good? What message? She finally understood what all of it meant.

Her daughter was returned to them, by the grace of God, and she was now joining her family just as they had celebrated for years without her. Vasilo's prayers, for all those days and weeks and years, were answered. All the candles she had lit, hoping for the one thing she wanted most desperately, wanted more than anything else, and that was her child, her first born, healthy, happy, and returned.

As a group, the family, Zacharis and Vasilo, Dena and Christos, Popi and brother Giorgos, the children, Costa and Nicko, and their other grandparents, Maria and Costas together holding hands, arms wrapped around one another, made their way slowly to a church that was filled already with parishioners. In fact, it was a little more crowded than usual. That night marked a significant Easter for which they all wanted to give thanks.

Dena remembered the first time she walked through the thick wooden doors of *Kimisis Tis Theotokou*, a church named for Christ's mother, Mary. It is a huge structure, comparatively, and dominant, a cornerstone of the village, which seems to greet visitors as they enter Kastania. For a shy person who never wanted to be noticed or made a fuss over, all eyes were on her, the center of attention. She was aware that people were staring, not to be rude, but to bear witness to one of the happiest occasions the village had ever experienced. She looked at the cold stone floor mostly, occasionally stealing glances, meeting some eyes that were fixated on her. She smiled.

The service had begun as the priest turned to the faithful. "Blessed is our God always, now and ever, and to the ages of ages. Amen. Glory to You, our God. Glory to You. Heavenly King, Comforter, Spirit of Truth, present in all places and filling all things, treasury of good things and giver of life: come; take Your abode in us; cleanse us of every stain, and save our souls, O Good one."

The lighting in the nave was low and muted.

The incense was thick and pungent as clouds of fragrance wafted from the thurible, the *thymiato*, the vessel that holds charcoal, frankincense, myrrh, and rose.

The canters, the *psaltes*, were in long black robes and miters.

They prayed: "Holy God, Holy Mighty, Holy Immortal, have mercy on us. Glory to the Father and the Son and the Holy Spirit. Both now and ever and to the ages of ages. Amen. All-holy Trinity, have mercy on us. Lord, forgive our sins. Master, pardon our transgressions. Holy One, visit and heal our infirmities for your name's sake. Lord, have mercy. Lord, have mercy."

The priests were adorned in black with purple-accented *epitrachelions*, the sashes that run down the front of their vestments, in the color of those still in mourning. The people were anticipating the arrival of a new day, a day filled with hope for better things to come. They anticipated, as Orthodox Christians had every year for millennia, the light that comes after the darkness.

Dena's nerves had calmed. She was deep into the service now, fully feeling what her life had been, how it had unfolded, and where she was on this night and with whom. It was as if the whole of her life was being revealed to her, including at this very moment for which she gave thanks as the priest said: "Savior, when You extended Your hands, You united things that had been divided. By Your confinement in the shroud and the sepulcher, You set free those who were fettered."

Her eyes filled with tears. She looked at her father, whose eyes had been a continual, ever-present well of water whenever he looked at her, and since he had seen her for the first time. In a way, she had been saved, she realized, and she was set free by a union that she never could have dreamed of because she was denied her own life's truth. It had been shrouded in darkness and was now given breath and light. Her thoughts, free and floating, were suddenly re-directed by the back and forth of the priest and canter. "Lift up your gates, ye princes, and be lifted up, ye everlasting doors; and the King of Glory shall come in." The canter responded, "Who is this King of Glory?" The priest answered, "The Lord, strong and mighty. The Lord mighty in battle. The Lord of the power. He is the King of Glory."

The time had come. It wouldn't be long now as the priest changed into a white vestment while every light in the church was extinguished. The parishioners were huddled together, Dena's family particularly close. It seemed that every one of them wanted to touch Dena in some way, somehow as they waited in the darkness, in the eerie silence. The people were completely still. Then, the muted sounds of movement, the heavy garments of the priest, shifting.

Finally, one flickering tiny light from a single candle emerged from behind the gilded gates of the sanctuary. It was in the hand of the priest. His other hand was holding a staff, the crosier, the *paterissa*. He said loudly and with conviction as the light from his candle was passed to all the others: "Come receive the light; and glorify Christ who has risen from the dead. Christ is risen. *Christos Anesti!*"

The light was exchanged, one person with the one next

to them, as gradually the church was fully aglow, bathed in a carpet of golden light, which reflected up and around through the windows in the dome suspended high above the people. It seemed as if a cloak of brightness had enveloped the entire tiny village of Kastania that night, a light so bright that in that moment it felt like it might have illuminated the entire world.

"Christ is risen from the dead, by death trampling upon death, and to those in the tombs He has granted life. Rejoice. *Christos Anesti*," proclaimed the priest. He raised his candle as he faced his flock.

"*Alithos Anesti*." Truly he has risen the parishioners answered together in response, and in unison they raised their arms and their candles toward the priest and toward heaven.

Dena's family, her husband and children, siblings, parents and in-laws stood together in the glow of that light, in the warmth of that church, with their friends, aunts and uncles, and cousins, all there to witness a union restored. An injustice made right. Pain now vanquished. Lives made whole.

They left the service amid a crush of people wanting to express an extraordinary welcome to Dena and her family from America, their love and support, and their hope for a future together for many years to come. The hour was late and it was time to break their 40-day lenten fast as the dozens of families broke apart for their respective homes, and a longer night ahead of eating, drinking, and the sunrise of a new day and new year.

Rejoice.

The village was particularly alive in the days that followed. There were more people there than usual, who had come from other villages in the area— Amarandos, Konitsa, Klidonia, Elatis. Friends. Friends of friends. Relatives. Kastania was preparing to celebrate the arrival of Dena Poulias and her family.

Zacharis had known many people over the years, who had heard him play, who knew his story, and who knew his family. He always had been supportive through their sorrows, joys, and their own struggles. With his *clarino,* Zacharis had been there to play with his band for all their celebrations. Now it was their turn to return the gesture by gathering to mark the good fortune and blessings bestowed upon their friend and on the Papazacharis family. It had been a long time coming.

The *plateia* was being transformed. A makeshift stage was being constructed. Tiny lights on cords were being strung around and across the square. Wooden tables and chairs were being pulled from every home and business for the *glendi*, the party that was to come.

The smell of food cooking billowed and punctuated the air coming from different corners of the village. Lamb on spits. Freshly baked pita. Garlic. Roasted vegetables. *Spanakopites*, spinach pies. *Tyropites*, cheese pies. Every woman in the village was in the kitchen preparing to share the bounty later that night. Others were baking sweets for the communal village feast. Kastania smelled like a veritable herbal garden like it does every spring. The fragrances from oregano, basil, rosemary, and thyme floated from patchwork gardens scattered in yards, along the roads, and growing wild in the surrounding fields.

The boys, Costa and Nicko, got very comfortable in the village and with their new-found family. They made friends easily with the other children, and ran around as free and as happy as they had ever been. "We hardly saw them," Christos said. "And we didn't worry about where they were, either." This was home and there were dozens of new relatives to make sure they didn't get into any mischief with their friends. It was idyllic and something so different from their lives in the United States.

Their new grandparents were delighted that the boys had so quickly adapted. They spoiled them, making up for the years they had lost. Their births. Their being able to help Dena. Their being able to serve as grandparents. Five of their birthdays.

Vasilo could not help herself as they ran, darting here and there. She would grab one or the other or both to hug them, kiss them, smiling as they ran off again, catching up to the other children.

It was the happiest Vasilo and Zacharis had ever been, they thought. Not that they were not delighted when their other children were born or about their other children, generally. Of course, they were. It was just that now their whole family was back together. Their first born was returned to them. The family was complete. The siblings together. And they were joined by the children of their child, a son-in-law, and his parents. Life, they thought, was good. Very good.

The couple could not keep their eyes off of Dena. It was as if, had they looked away, if even for a few minutes, that she might disappear. The moments looking at her were so sweet, so precious. They inhaled the nearness of her. They would hold her hand, touch her face, stroke her hair—small, gentle gestures of how much they loved her and had missed her. Dena wanted to be physically close to them, too, although it felt surreal. Their existence, although unknown to her for so many years, was gradually made vivid and by their very real presence and affection.

Vasilo and Zacharis were concerned that Dena knew and understood that they had tried and wanted to find her, but every trace of her had been destroyed. There was no trail to her, no lead of any kind. They wanted her to understand and to know that she had never been forgotten. They felt guilt. Also, they carefully asked questions about her life with her adoptive parents, without pushing. Dena told them only the basics. "I couldn't tell them the truth," she said. "It would have been too painful for them, after all they had suffered already. And what did it matter? Nick and Amelia were dead. They didn't need to know, and I didn't want to relive it in the re-telling anyway."

Dena wanted to be in this moment. She found herself intently looking at each parent. She studied their faces, their gestures, and realized that she could see fragments of herself in each of them. The exuberance and lively spirit of her mother. The quiet, soulful depth of her father. She was struck by their love for each other, survivors through such harrowing, painful times. They had fought to be together, and so many times could have been ripped apart, pressured into conformity, beaten into submission. They had not relented and had so valiantly resisted the influence of others as they were determined to remain steadfast, and together. Theirs was a great love story, she thought.

Dena was drawn to Zacharis in a way she had never experienced before. Daughter for father. He was quiet and strong. Gentle and kind. Warm. Loving. Proud to be her Dad. Her *Baba*. She would sit close to him now. He would wrap his arm around her to the back of the chair. She would lay her hand on his leg. The strength of their feelings, unspoken, would draw their heads together. Leaning. Lingering. Deep breaths. Taking in the moment of having found each other, of being together. At last.

"Whenever he looked at me," Dena recalled, "I could actually feel how much he loved me. Just in that look. His eyes said it all. Every time. His eyes would well with tears. They didn't fall. They were just soaked. We didn't have to say a word. I knew. He knew." Zacharis never fully understood that he was the father Dena had longed for, that she had needed, since she was a little girl. But he was with her now, and it was all that mattered.

The celebration in Kastania lasted for three days. It was an extraordinary homecoming party, a *glendi*, befitting the occasion. Dena greeted as many people as she could. Others came to her. It was a whirlwind of socializing, the by-product of which was crying and laughter and love. Pure love.

As he had done hundreds of times before, Zacharis gathered the band together, his boys, and took to the stage.

Everyone knew this band. Everyone loved this band and the way Zacharis played his *clarino*. There was restless anticipation as the band tuned their instruments. A flood of notes, up and down the musical scale, came from Zacharis as he loosened his mouth, tongue, and lips for the hours he would play this night.

He began with a familiar rift. Just the *clarino*, at first, setting up the song. It was familiar. It was a <u>*tsamiko*</u>.

Dena Poulias loved to dance.

The crowd encouraged her to take to the floor at the front of a line that was growing. That night she danced like she had never danced before.

Kefi.

Christos tucked himself away, to the back of the crowd, and watched his wife. This night was all about her. He had never seen her quite like this. So happy, finally home, having found her place. He couldn't stop smiling. The place erupted in applause.

Vasilo came to Dena, took her hand, and, for the first time, they danced, mother and daughter. It was one of those moments the village would never forget. They had each loved to dance all their lives. And they were each so good at it. But tonight, they would dance together for the first time. Again, a loud, audible rush from the villagers, who were overwhelmed by the scene.

And then, in a moment both uncharacteristic and unexpected, Zacharis laid down his clarinet and signaled with a wave that someone should take his place. He stepped down from the stage and walked through the thick, woven line of dancers, with deliberation and purpose, making his way to his wife and daughter. Before he even got there, the reaction from the villagers swelled into a wave of applause and whistles that was carried up into the night air like the embers from a bonfire that burst into the night sky, as the three of them took center stage. Wedging himself between them, he took each of their hands in his, drawing one, then the other to his lips, tenderly kissing each.

And together they danced.

They danced.

May 5, 2000.

It was Dena's 42th birthday, a day her parents never forgot, but it was the first birthday she celebrated with them, so her mother carried in a cake with a single lit candle. The small house was packed with relatives. Dena's face glowed as that one tiny, flickering flame seemed to light up her entire face. She closed her eyes and decided to say a prayer as she blew out the candle. Her mother grabbed her face and smothered it with kisses as she would a child on her first birthday.

Dena didn't need to make a wish because it had already come true.

Post-Script

Today Dena and Christos Poulias live in Estero, Florida. They own and operate the popular eatery the Mykonos Kuzina restaurant in Naples.

Their sons, Costa and Nicko, also live in Florida, near their parents. Costa helps out at the restaurant when he can, but has gone back to school to become a nurse, which has been a long-time ambition. Nicko is in charge of the kitchen at the restaurant and puts in long hours with his parents.

For over 20 years now, the Papazacharis family has been reunited. They have remained close and in touch, visiting each other as often as possible.

Popi, Dena's sister, is now an American citizen and moved to Florida to help at the restaurant. For now, she lives with her sister and brother-in-law.

Brother Giorgos is married and the father of two children. He and his family live in Trikala, Greece.

Apostolos "Zacharis" Papazacharis died on December 15, 2020. Dena and Popi flew to Greece for the funeral and to be with their mother.

Dena said, "You know I feel robbed. Robbed for his absence in my life for all those years. And robbed now because he died and I wanted more years with him. I have realized that so much about him is who I am. His love of music. Dancing. The clarinet. I never knew who I was, why I was who I am, until not very long ago. Until I knew him.

It's just so sad. I have cried so much. I don't know if I have any more tears left."

Zacharis's lonely *clarino*? It was buried with him.

And as for all those hundreds of letters, exchanged between Zachari and Vasilo over twelve years while he was in prison, they are in a locked trunk, which, to date, Vasilo is unwilling to share with anyone.

ACKNOWLEDGEMENTS

There would have been no novella were it not for Kathy Kearns and Dena Poulias. I met Kathy, Dena's cousin, in a Greek-language class in Oakland, California. She told me about Dena's incredible story and introduced us. I asked Dena if I could write about her, and over the course of a year, interviewed her, her husband and sister. I applaud her for her courage because I know how difficult it was for her to conjure up so many painful memories, but she saw purpose in it. My deep gratitude to the Poulias and Papazacharis families for understanding the importance of Dena's story, its place in the global adoption narrative, and the fight for ethical, open adoption practices.

My eternal thanks to Gonda Van Steen, one of the world's leading modern Greek studies scholars and author of the seminal *Adoption, Memory and Cold War Greece: Kid Pro Quo?* It was from this exhaustive study that I referenced and put into historical context Dena's story. Gonda has taught me more about the dark, painful history of Greece and also my own place in it as an adoptee. She has become a dear, trusted friend and has helped me in my own search for my biological roots as she has with hundreds of other adoptees around the world.

My enduring appreciation for journalist and best-selling author, Gabrielle Glaser, and her incredible book, *American Baby*, which further educated me about the same, awful adoption practices in America, which happened years ago and are still happening here in the United States today. Her book tapped into my own heart and helped me to both acknowledge and express my feelings about my own adoption. Also, now a dear friend, I cherish her caring ways, generosity, sensitivity, and good humor.

To my first readers, my oldest and dearest friends from Gary, Indiana, Beth Pappas Orfanos and Pam Bianchi Schrode, who have been reading the things I have written since our days in high school when I was a journalist for our newspaper. Both of their reactions to my first draft of this story told me that I was on to something. Their friendship and love for over 50 years now means the world.

What a joy it has been to know these people: Cindy Kanellis, Kathy Kearns (again), Meagan Travlos, and Colleen Amick Giapitsoglou, my Greek-language school classmates, who have been such vocal supporters of my work and such fun to be with as we learn together a language we love. Thank you all for the time you took to read my essays about adoption, for your friendship, and for all the laughter.

Thanks to these inspirational adoptee activists who are teaching me more every day about the impact of adoption on children and the adults they become: Greg Luce and Lynelle Long. I have such gratitude and respect for all you do on our behalf.

To Andrew Mossin, professor, poet and author of *A Son from the Mountains*, my fellow Greek-born adoptee, my brother, for his advice, support, and his kindness.

And finally, to Francesca Fifis, who is always eager and willing to read every word I have ever written over and over again. She is patient, a thoughtful editor, sounding board, and honest reviewer of my work. She has been by my side as I returned to my own adoption search after 21 years of dormancy. My life would not be what it is without her.

MARY CARDARAS holds a PhD in Public and International Affairs from Northeastern University and a Master of Science degree in Journalism from Northwestern University. She is Associate Professor and Chair of Communication at California State University, East Bay, where she teaches journalism and political communication.

She has been a news producer, journalist, and documentary filmmaker for over 40 years. Currently, she produces documentary shorts about the effects of the environment on public health. She is also creating the Demos Center Project, a program for university students who are interested in studying the intersectionality of democracy, public policy, a free press, rhetoric and leadership, which will be based in Athens, Greece.

Cardaras is herself a Greek-born adoptee of the 1950's. She was placed in an Athens orphanage nine days after her birth and later was in two foster homes before being taken by her maternal adoptive grandparents by ship to New York and then to her adoptive parents in the Midwest. She learned about the story of Dena Poulias through Dena's adoptive cousin during Greek language school, based at a church in Oakland, California. She has become an activist for adoptees around the world in their fight for ethical adoption practices, open records, original birth certificates, and citizenship of origin for those who want it.

Cardaras grew up in a large Greek community in Gary, Indiana and later traversed the country producing news in seven major markets. Today she lives in Sonoma, California.